AQUARIUS

THE BOOK OF LIFESTYLE DESIGN

COURT REINLAND

Copyright © 2019 by Court Reinland Inc.

courtreinland.com

ISBN: 1-950260-00-3

ISBN-13: 978-1-950260-00-3

CONTENTS

1. Seeds	1
2. Five Areas of Major Dysfunction	5
3. Disconnect of People and the Environment	7
4. Disconnect of People and Education	17
5. Disconnect of People and Work	21
6. Disconnect of People and Family	27
7. Disconnect of People and Government	29
8. Socialism is Failing	43
9. How do we get there from here?	53
10. Aquarius Quickstart Guide	65
11. Safe and Stable No Matter the Weather	73
12. Towards Greater Harmony	81
13. Charity is good, self-sufficiency is better	85
14. Closing Comments	87
15. FAQS	91
16. Community Examples	99
17. The Exchange System	103
18. Post Script	107

To my family, who always stood by me while I was writing this book. And to my spiritual teacher, Shifu Li Hongzhi, without whom I would have been unable to enlighten to the material I have come up with in this book.

"And shall pass away this vicious age of Mars and shall come the age of Aquarius."

1
SEEDS

~

"The lucky few who can be involved in creative work of any sort will be the true elite of mankind, for they alone will do more than serve a machine."
- *Isaac Asimov (prediction in 1964 of the world to come)*

THERE IS A SEED SPROUTING, a sense that life is about to change. A sense of a shift in consciousness, and many, regardless of the diversity of their different beliefs, can feel it. Something big is coming, something larger and greater than the scope of this book, but toward which this book tends and premeditates.

Truly, as we have come to the modern time, the human condition feels more and more in the service of a machine, though not quite a literal one. A machine which is the system of modern life that dehumanizes even as it provides, that stifles even as it grows, that kills even as it need not.

Asimov predicted a world with less work, owing to the abundance of automation, with boredom as a result. In truth, we have achieved boredom but ironically, and sadly, we are also now saddled with the tedium of ever more work.

We have come upon the worst of both worlds, but it need not be this way. We have on the earth, the most intelligent, most colorful, most diverse, and most spiritually awake people who may have ever inhabited it. But we have yet to do one thing: to work together harmoniously.

Yet there is a force now growing, in the hearts and minds of people the world over, thriving in the hearts of the makers, the organic growers, the life hackers, the farmacists, the self-educators, the coders and cryptographers, the independent thinkers, and the philosophers and the artists and people of all unnamed kinds.

That force is *lifestyle design*.

The ability to live one's life together with one's peers in a manner that we the people *want*, not merely what has been left to us by history or forced upon us by the powers that be.

It is only that we have yet to realize how easily this vision can become a reality, that we only need stretch forth our hands and take it. There doesn't need to be a violent revolution, no hard-fought struggle or war, for the lifestyle designer has abandoned these outdated and backward mental philosophies of violence, using instead only the peaceful but skillful methods of their mind, their reason, their science and their spirit, making dinosaurs, not enemies, of the systems that encumber them.

First the good news: abundance is real. The good news is, the natural systems of the earth can provide more than enough for a life of sustenance and happiness for all.

If you have an idea and a few friends, you can change your life.

The philosophy of struggle, which is the mentality that one must always compete, that one must gain at the disadvantage of another, is false.

What you are viewing is unique in that it is both a book and an app. The app is the functional object, whereas the book is the explanation and philosophical justification for its use. This app allows anyone to create their own community corporation or "lifestyle design community," to create bilaws for that community, create their own fiat currency, using blockchain or "cryptocurrency" technology, and cooperate and live autonomously with their fellow human beings. If the reader can grasp the value of that, they may proceed directly to the "Aquarius Quickstart Guide" section of the book. But first the *why*.

2

FIVE AREAS OF MAJOR DYSFUNCTION

THE SYSTEMS that govern the world, including the natural systems of the world itself, are on the verge of collapse. The effects may not yet be apparent, but they are apparent to some. Having raced off the cliff, we are now in a free fall, but we have not yet hit the bottom. The areas that are broken are many, but principally, there are five: 1. Disconnect of people and the environment 2. Disconnect of people and education 3. Disconnect of people and work 4. Disconnect of people and family 5. Disconnect of people and government.

∽

FOR THE SAKE of our families, our children, the future of the environment and the planet, we ***must act***.

3

DISCONNECT OF PEOPLE AND THE ENVIRONMENT

∼

AT THE TURN of the 20th century, over 70% of the world population was directly employed in agriculture. Now, only 3% of the world population is. Yet, we have a food surplus. That really is a great statistic. It means that our production capability outstrips our need by many orders of magnitude. This means we are producing more than enough for everyone with less human effort. Thank you, machines.

So, we have developed into a paradigm that is actually good - at least, it is good from one angle. We currently produce more than we need. There is more food produced every year by an order anywhere from 10%-50%, according to varying different estimates. The reason people starve globally is not a question of actual capability; it is one of distribution, waste, political intrigue, outright war, and corruption. *There is no actual food supply shortage.*

A recent report by the UN stated the only way to ensure the

long-term food stability of the planet was local scale organic farming. Not GMOs as many thought, and not massive centralized distribution, but local scale organic farming. A lot of food spoils as it is transported, and it has to be heavily preserved by pesticides or other chemicals, with one statistic saying the average piece of food travels over 3000 miles before it reaches our plates. This itself is a problem and vastly inefficient, with a lot of resources wasted in fuel, time, transit, and unnecessary labor. Let alone the environmental repercussions of so many chemicals, greenhouse gas emissions, etc.

Beyond this, there are also numerous health problems in our modern food system. Obesity is on the rise in almost every nation of the world, and countries where the so-called fast food chains have been introduced have seen the fastest increases over their historical averages.

Much of the food we eat has been heavily modified from its natural condition. Foods are processed and stripped of their inherent nutrients, made into the so-called junk food and even the raw constituents: fruits, vegetables, meats and dairy; many have been hybridized or raised in such a way as to maximize production or profit, not health. Health is not the primary goal of the supplier, because emphasis has only been placed on one variable: money, not on the other factors of a balanced lifestyle. This is to say nothing even of genetic modification (GMOs) whose introduction some cite as being correlated with a rise in other health disorders. So, there is a disconnect, with many modern people not knowing what foods are healthy for them, nor how to cook them (or not cook them, as the case may be) or where to obtain them. There is a broad and worldwide disconnect between people and food.

According to the U.S. Department of Agriculture (USDA), nearly 85 percent of every dollar you spend at the grocery store goes toward paying for processing and marketing of the food. A mere 15 percent goes to the farmer who actually grows the food.

Lifestyle design allows for a very simple organizational structure whereby members of a community can participate in their own farming and food production and share it with others. Having recruited a few farmers, chefs, or food makers into the community, and having crowdfunded a plot of arable land, one can easily leverage simple permaculture or even more advanced technologies like hydroponics to produce food by and for the group. There are already groups in Sweden, and in other countries at the time of this writing, that have created very unique and creative groups around food. One such group is Plantagon, with their World Food Tower project.

Another effort, called the Global Village Construction Set, produced by the Open Source Ecology Project, is a set of machines and blueprints and parts for machines that can do all the tasks related to sustaining a community, including food production and housing production site preparation. They even have machines that can make other machines. All open source. So, the resources are there, and if a community has enough willing participants, they can be had and built. Dreams can be achieved with lifestyle design.

The reason this is so necessary is because modern agriculture and food processing of the modern world is currently producing a systematic state of "unhealth." Obesity is epidemic the world over and many disorders such as autism spectrum, diabetes, Alzheimer's, heart attacks, and cancer are dramatically on the rise.

Despite supposedly advanced science and modern medicine, these issues are all still rising, some at an alarming rate. It is the position of this book that at least some of the cause, perhaps a large portion of the cause, lies in the fact that humans have become so disconnected from the origin of their food and consumption of food in its natural and organic state, with many in inner city environments having no affordable access to fresh fruit or vegetables at all. A recent article in the *New York Times,* and also appearing in the book *Food Wars,* shows that much of modern food is hybridized, to say nothing even of processing, let alone GMOs. Hybridized food, that is, food that has been bred away from its original condition by plant breeding, contains only a tenth or sometimes only a thousandth of the original micronutrients of its heirloom ancestors.

Not only that, but when you talk about things like processed food and fast food, food that is prepared far beyond how it occurs in nature, you run into all kinds of spurious and questionable practices. Take for example food engineering. There are people, truly engineers, right now at the major food companies, at the major agribusiness companies who are designing and engineering the food we eat. They are designing it to taste a way they think people will like, but they are also designing things like "mouth feel," adding ingredients - many chemicals, truly - that do things like make a person not feel full, make a person crave more food, subtly addict a person to the food, and so on. This is not a secret, and there is much publicly available literature documenting how and in what ways this is happening. The health risks of doing all this are still a question of debate, but there are many signs and correlations with the rise of certain health conditions broadly that seem to indicate we are heading in a very wrong direction.

Saving aside health risks and other environmental and philosophical factors, there is still the issue of cost. Food costs a lot! It may be relatively affordable where you live, or it may not, but it certainly costs more than it needs to, especially considering the earth produces food from nature for free. A recent estimate of modern packaged (processed) and retail (fast) food estimated that 70% of the cost of food is marketing, packaging, and transportation. Meaning that food, broadly, could cost ⅓ of what it does. So, the essential labour of producing food, the farming itself, is only ⅓ of the cost. With lifestyle design, the farm could inherently be local to the community, or even if it was remote, by necessity of the living location of the members of the lifestyle design community, you would only be looking at the cost of delivering it directly to the members, as many CSAs have done.

Let's take a typical small farmer as an example, and then expand to how an agribusiness operates, and you can see for yourself how there is waste. More will be explained in the *Community Examples* section of this book, but let's look at this simple example for now. Let's look at the simple farmer's costs and challenges. Assume the farmer was born with or is lucky enough to own his own piece of arable land. He decides to grow simple vegetable crops on his land. He can't do it all himself, so he hires a few neighborhood people and some relatives to work for him, plus his own children. Now, he needs equipment, which is expensive. He takes out a loan to buy a tractor and some processing machinery. He then sees that the price of the vegetables he intends to sell at the grocery store are pretty competitive; they aren't low, but they aren't sky-high either, so he'll have to be really efficient in the operation and pay people very minimally. It becomes harvest time. The weather was decent, so the yield is ok but smaller than he anticipated. He has his crop, but whoops, he didn't think of how to distribute it. He doesn't have any retailers booked in advance, so he hires a salesperson and business manager to go find some. Now he knows he'll have to charge more for the produce, but he will still have thin margins.

He hires some more people, and now he's got sales, marketing and PR people to help, but there's a problem: he hasn't got any cash left to pay for it all, so he approaches a bank and some venture capitalists and now he's got money. But that money came with strings attached. He's got to have a board, and he's got to do things the way his backers say because, after all, it's their money. The people he's had to hire aren't cheap, and he's got to keep making a large profit every year to pay everyone and to keep his shareholders happy. On top of that, his competitors have been doing the same, so now he has to work extra hard. He has to research what his customers want and to try to develop products that match their tastes.

Now, as you probably can tell, that small farmer has become a full-blown agri-business. And that's reflected in the price of the products. Not only that, but he has made a few sacrifices along the way. He is paying the workers less than what they are worth, even less than they can really afford to live on, and while he started out organic, he found that the pests were really too pesky, so he had to start using some pesticides. When the GMO seed salesman came by promising

25% greater yields, well... though he regrets it more and more now, he didn't say no. Such are the necessities, we're told, of doing business *at scale*.

Can you really blame him? At first, the simple farmer just wanted to feed his family, and later, he wanted to leave a legacy and set an example of hard work for his children. A lot of agribusinesses - even ones with highly questionable ethics and practices today - started out as small family farmers. They didn't do anything illegal, they didn't screw anyone to get where they are now - yet the environment is a mess, the workers still struggle to own even a modest house, and your food is expensive with many new studies every day showing that it's poisoning you and slowly making you fat.

So, what's to blame? It's just the machine. It's one of only a few routes left to a person who wishes to succeed in modern *late-stage* capitalism. Everyone faces the same choices. And who's to say - would you, dear reader - as revolutionary as you are - would you truly make choices that were much different had you been in their shoes?

Lifestyle design doesn't eliminate these ethical choices. Those will always be with us. Greed will always be with us. But lifestyle design does eliminate some of the conditions that necessitate such choices. Let's take a look.

In a typical *lifestyle design community* (or *community corporation*, if you want), the stakeholders are all the same. The people consuming are the same as the people producing, and they are the owners themselves. So for one thing, there's no need to advertise, because you all know each other, and you know what you're doing; it's just a matter of choosing what to produce for yourselves (you can even vote on it!). It also eliminates competition, because a lifestyle community is a closed loop, a closed ecosystem, an inward facing corporation that only sells to itself. You don't have to overcome *everyone else*. You just have to overcome the challenges of production - make it as *time efficient* for everyone as possible. The goal here is *enough sustenance* for *minimum work*, not *maximum production* for *cost-profitable work* as is the paradigm in speculative capitalism (ordinary outward facing corporations).

Then you add automation. The same kind of process and physical automation is at work in a typical capitalist company: machines, computers and routines. You don't even need the most advanced kind, not to start out anyways. Remember, the earth yields up food for free. The sun gives its energy for free. There's only that little bit of work that needs to be done to get it there, to organize it and get it to your plate. So, as long as your community has ownership of a piece of arable land, you can begin. From there, the advantages multiply. Now, if you've started with a lot of capital, the agriculture machines can do nearly everything (and it can still be organic food). But, let's say you don't have that much capital, maybe you just have a few people and only a few bitcoins in the bank. Then you would start by merely organizing the labor among the available participants - like an Israeli Kibbutz might. Regular capitalism uses division and specialization of labor, management, and automation to achieve scale. A lifestyle designer would also use division and specialization of labor, management, and automation, but he would achieve *efficiency* instead of *scale*. And we aren't talking about 1960s *communalism* (though there's nothing wrong with that). I'm not saying everyone has to be subsistence farmers with long hair and tie-dyed shirts. There will still be division of labor, and there will still be choice of labor, there will still be *doing what you love,* but it will be easier, it will be more efficient, it will be less competitive, and less wasteful, and far more sustainable and more harmonious than current methods. More on this later, but now let's look at another area of major dysfunction.

4

DISCONNECT OF PEOPLE AND EDUCATION

∽

THERE IS a shocking statistic making the rounds of late, and any anecdotal survey of the people around you will prove its correctness: 70% of people are employed in a field unrelated to their college major. Archaeology? Good for you! How's the coffee shop sound? Philosophy major? Well, you can discuss it with the fares in your cab. Communications? How does retail sound? (Everything is communication, right?) Library Science? Welcome to the unemployment line, baby!

Many of today's young people emerge from the cocoon of college saddled with thousands if not tens or hundreds of thousands of dollars of debt. Yet employers still regularly lament a "skills gap," saying, "It's just so hard to find good people." It's clear the system is broken, but what's broken about it?

For starters, majors are self-chosen by students, not dictated by actual economic need. The availability of jobs has no bearing or relationship to the majors people choose. It's the inevitable outcome of capitalist economics and free choice. There's bound to be a disconnect. It's like throwing darts in the dark, or a better analogy would be roulette. Sure, you can improve your odds by choosing all red or all black instead of a specific number, just like you can major in what you think will be a growing field, but it doesn't guarantee a match. Most people are just majoring in what they like, following the advice of the old self-help saw, *"Do what you love, and the money will follow."* And why shouldn't they? You don't want to force people to do something they don't want to do, right? But it doesn't guarantee there's a job at the end, so there's a disconnect there.

I'm not blaming universities for this. It's not that universities are doing a terrible job educating people, though some are a bit overpriced nowadays for the result you get. There's actually not much they can do under the current model; it's an issue of *diminishing returns*. In the early days, a college degree was prestigious because few people had them. Most people were laborers, so if you had one, you really stood out. But now he has one, and she has one too, and every single person has one, so the field is again level. If you don't have one, it's almost like people brand you as unintelligent or think you're some kind of social misfit. So, you have to have one—that's the perception anyways, but the actual lived effect is diminishing; as some people facetiously say, "It's a gold stamp on your high school diploma." Plus, you're a few thousand in debt, still standing at the starting line.

The way of the future is continuous education in a light, flexible way, well into adulthood. And self-education as well. Technology and the internet have literally put millions of educational resources at your fingertips, and many of them are free.

Lifestyle design takes this a step further by coordinating education with actual community need, thus solving the dissociated work/education relationship problem.

With lifestyle design, people can continuously improve themselves in a coordinated way and continuously master new skills. Remembering that with each iteration or cycle of community development, the previously mastered skills or tasks have become easier to do, so there's more time available to learn new ones.

Let's address this by way of example. Say you have a group of twenty people, and you all have some shared ideas in common and you want to start a community. You decide to start with the basics: food production and simple sustenance. You've decided to select "basic democracy" from the drop-down menu in the Aquarius software. So. in the first vote, it was decided that some equipment would be purchased with the seed money in the group's bank. Forty acres of land was purchased and sown, enough to provide food for the twenty members. In the first year, it took Sherry 20 hours a week to seed everything. Will spent 10 hours a week weeding, and when harvest time came, Anna spent 15 hours a week picking. Tim will spend 25 hours at the end to prep and present everything at the community market. These numbers are arbitrary of course, but the concept is not. While this was going on, three other members had been appointed to a research committee and had spent 17 hours a week during that year researching how to do agriculture, so that at the next iteration of the cycle, it only takes Sherry 5 hours, Will 2, and Anna 3 using machinery, and in the next iteration, automation was used and so on. In 5 years' time, with the cycles of development, everyone's working time was reduced to 9 days a year—*9 days a year,* not per month. Such is the ultimate efficiency possible in lifestyle design. Imagine what could be possible with all the free time, the things the members in the community could study, or write and the charitable work they could do or the travel time they could have, or simply all the time they could spend with their families.

Think about it, the most brilliant minds of our generation, working furiously only to serve our most basic needs, or even worse the trivial: yet another messaging app, or an indexed organizer for cat videos that sorts by type of cat. Needs that could easily be met under a different system. So much wasted effort! Just think of problems that could be solved if people were freed from the rat race, the medicines that could be invented, the cosmos explored, world hunger, an endless list of problems that could be solved! Yet humanity is shackled in its infancy. Well, I am trying to unshackle them!

5

DISCONNECT OF PEOPLE AND WORK

∽

You know that it is happening. You feel in your bones that it is happening, but you may or may not be able to describe it. You are putting in ever more effort and getting ever less back. Does that sound accurate? Or maybe you are underemployed, forever on edge about any accident or circumstance that may disrupt your fragile financial existence. You might have had to rely ever more on credit, even for your basic necessities.

Capitalism, as Marx before pointed out, can be a very destructive machine. Or, one may say, a rather binary machine, that both produces and destroys at the same time.

Capitalist corporations, as everyone knows, are just money machines. They are set up principally, and by charter, to return the maximum value to their shareholders. They can be other things, and of course, they have to add value to people's lives in some way via their goods and services. But the main goal is clear: it's just money.

But people, when surveyed, don't value just money. They do value money, but they also value health, learning, freedom, the environment, time with their family, spirituality, and a whole host of other interests and hobbies. Yet the dominant paradigm values them for only one thing: their productive capacity. Enter lifestyle design.

Like a milling machine run amok - at one time useful for food but with a world of wheat before it - capitalism will just grind and grind and grind, until everything is ground into dust. Humans fundamentally are not built for the pace of constant change that has come over them in the last 200 years or so since the industrial, and now information revolutions, and when the pace of change or its perception becomes too fast or too unbearable, people will - as recent elections in some places have shown - crave it's opposite: safety, stability, and security.

The binary economy - divided into two layers - the sustainability layer and the speculative layer. Think of the speculative layer, which is what we have now, just that one layer. A person can start with a little bit of capital, have an idea and start their own business. They can build an electric car, farm organic food, or send a rocket to the moon. Better widget, better mousetrap, and the market will reward you for your productivity. If I need a job, I can find one. If you need a worker, you can hire me and pay me for my labor. If I need something, I go to your shop or another shop and buy it. People everywhere say this is a pretty efficient system, but from an engineering or systems theory perspective, capitalism is far from the MOST efficient system that can be designed.

Think about a typical corporation now, a modern brand.

Massive amounts of money are spent on two things: data and marketing. Corporations have to work really hard to find out what their customers want. Customers don't necessarily want to interact with corporations because they know they will try to sell them something. Sometimes, customers don't know what they want when asked directly. They only know it when they see something, and their desire is aroused. This leads us to our second area where modern corporations massively spend, which is marketing. Since humankind's essential needs, as we discussed above, are already met, most of the productive capacity of the economy is trained on frivolous wants. These wants must be buoyed by marketing. No one needed all that pointless crap yesterday, nobody needs it today, but oh boy in comes the marketing, and soon, everybody wants it! I say this having worked for years on Madison Avenue (sinner that I am!). But the problem soon becomes that he's advertising too, and she's advertising too, and it costs more and more, so you need more and more data points gleaned through ever more invasive methods to target advertising more precisely and to keep the cost down.

People become cogs, plugging in at desks they don't own, in offices they don't like, with their existence reduced to a few simple metrics of performance. Rise above, and the machine will give you more cogs to manage; fall below, and the machine shears you off. The corporate grind. Of course, all this was made necessary by competition, the need to always be better, faster and stronger than the next guy. So first came analysis, then came systemization, then came automation, and your job became more like the computer itself. Of course, competition has created the multitude of modern conveniences, the abundance of modern life, the things that you and I enjoy, so it isn't all bad, right?

The problem is that it has run its course. Competition has run up against a kind of limit, whereby further refinement and improvement within the bounds of the current system simply leads to exhaustion and diminishing returns on the part of the worker, and gradually diminishing returns on the part of the corporation as a whole. This is called *late-stage capitalism*, and with it comes another challenge. Remember how we talked earlier about abundance being real? Well, at this stage, the market is already producing and meeting all the *real needs* people have, so new sectors and new ever-less-essential products and services need to be produced to maintain a path of growth. Growth is a set-in-stone requirement for normal capitalist companies and in-fact is a requirement for trading on any of the major stock exchanges as well. *You must be constantly growing.* Now, setting aside the first problem that this is in fact impossible and unsustainable within the current environment of the earth. (For how can everything constantly grow within a finite system?) Which is why now, no joke, corporations are looking to mine and colonize Mars, the moon, etc. because they know about this problem. But the second half of this problem is that there is less meaningful work that actually needs to be done. You need to eat and pay rent, so you need a job, but the system as a whole can run without you. Your input into it, your work, is not empirically necessary to the function of the whole. So, you are a cog, because a cog is the easiest and only thing left. Of course, you could start your own company, but 95% of businesses that start, fail. Over 540,00 businesses are started every year in the US; of those, 95% (99% if you're in the restaurant business) statistically will fail. And again, this is a result of the extra, unused capacity, eating itself. Like the plant sprouting through the crack in the pavement, you don't like the corporate jobs available to you, so you start your own, do your own thing. Nothing wrong with that, but it's hard, right? You have to get your name out there, you have to find clients, so you have to advertise, you have to learn skills outside your specialty, outside your major, outside what you really love to do. So, everyone learns photoshop, everyone becomes a marketer and advertising fills up every inch of space, every blank wall, every pause in conversation, even the placemat under your bowl of rice - more goddamn advertising. Is that really the right idea? Is that really the way life has to be? I say that it is not.

With lifestyle design, by nature, this becomes unnecessary. The customers and the workers and the owners are the same people. There is no need to collect all this data on people; you just ask people what they want. Once people have voted, let's say, if you're set up as a democracy, then those become the items that will be made. There is no need to market them because all the members are all there and they are aware through the Aquarius software of what's available. So, all the communication is just a circle; there's not all this need to broadcast information everywhere in hopes of picking up new buyers. You only need to ask people directly what they want and then give it to them. You can create the lifestyle you want, together with your peers, directly, in a closed loop system. All this leads us to our next disconnect.

6

DISCONNECT OF PEOPLE AND FAMILY

∽

OF ALL THE problems in our modern society, this is probably the most severe, the most noticeable and the most immediately relevant to most people. Many things, people who have not chosen to live an awakened life, may simply pass by, adrift as it were, not noticing their effects or consequences, and this can be said to apply to most other areas of disconnect. But family is hard to miss. We all have families, and sometimes the effects can be devastating and profound, and sometimes they can be subtler, but we are all affected by these. Let's take a couple examples. In America, you have this phenomenon, this term called "latchkey kids," and this is a term that people use for kids whose parents work so much that they aren't home when the children come home from school, so they leave the "key" out on the "latch," so the kids can let themselves into the house when they get home because there's no one else to do it for them. But this whole term is basically an explanation of the entire state, a common state people are in, wherein they have no time for their kids. Economic necessity has driven people to the maximum of their productive capacity, the maximum of their time capacity, and they have no room left for their kids. There is no time left to educate them, to raise them in a way that the parent thinks is right, to impart to them that important personal knowledge that they cannot get anywhere but home. So the kids are often left to the nanny or the babysitter or simply left to the TV or the smartphone or tablet or whatever because the parents are too busy. This in itself is a massive disconnect, and it's caused by and related to the other disconnects in other areas of life.

Because you have these really busy parents, you have kids who fill their time with whatever kind of entertainment is at hand, which can include crime or involvement with street gangs, if those things are present in the environment. Furthermore, because there's no time to cook, the children are eating prepackaged food or junk food and aren't having meals with the family, so their brains aren't functioning optimally because of the nutrition, and they also aren't receiving the attention, the emotional nourishment from those family bonds, that family time. Because there is no time, they don't have much time to help their children with their schoolwork if they need help, so they don't learn as well, and on and on and on. It doesn't take much extrapolation to see how these things also compound each other and how a problem in one can create a problem in the other. If this continues to compound in this way, the whole thing snowballs. The problems in all areas of life get worse as time goes on. This is a kind of fundamental, root problem.

7
DISCONNECT OF PEOPLE AND GOVERNMENT

Democracy is broken, but what replaces it?

DEMOCRACY IS BROKEN, but what can replace it? Having seen the undoing of the modern representative-democratic socio-capitalist societies, having seen them falter in even their basic functions and descend into the madness of soundbites and ad-hominem attacks, this is the question on people's minds. *But what can replace it?* What system, yet derived or designed, can mend its flaws while retaining its merits? This is the question. I would suggest that the answer, the next step in the evolution of prevailing ideologies, is *lifestyle design*.

The secret to undoing any corrupt government, as seen through historical observation, is by *not relying* on said government. It's not that the government as an abstract concept has power; it's that people grant it that power via belief. Even if objectively, the military really does have power over you via its weapons — yet, the military itself is made of people, and these people must believe in their right to that power and their allegiance to said government, or else the whole would descend into disorganized chaos. Even in the most corrupt and despotic regimes, some people believe in them, some people want what they have, depend on them, and support them. The failing of past revolutions happened because they merely replaced one kind of control with another. Under communism, for example, instead of power being measured by inherited wealth, class and the business acumen of private citizens and businesses, power became measured by closeness to positions of government power and hierarchy within the central government itself.

They failed to realize the fundamental truth that *organization always tends toward a pyramid*. From the monarchies of old to the bureaucracies of present day, hierarchy has always been with us, whether we like to admit it or not.

Democracy, by design, is inefficient. But its merit is that *it limits everyone*, so hypothetically, no one person obtains too much power, and thus abuse and corruption are limited.

Dictatorship and monarchy are very efficient. With just one person at the top, whatever they say goes. Simple. Of course, if that person becomes corrupt, it can be very dangerous.

At its core, a country is just an association, made of members, no different than the local Lion's Club or Rotary. Except, a country calls its members *citizens* instead of just *members*. They usually have a series of codified beliefs called laws and a bureaucracy to enforce them, including a type of military or police. But the basis is highly similar, whether talking about Switzerland or a Guinean tribe.

Of course, when a country is mentioned, people may attach a whole host of emotional or nationalistic feelings to it, whether on the basis of religion, ethnicity or shared history, but these feelings, while valid, have very little to do with the *logic* of running it or with the actual practical or pragmatic *actual* state of a country.

However, as can easily be observed, in the course of democracy, it is often these baser feelings that are played upon by politicians or unscrupulous members of the media. People are polarized, divided semiotically into opposing sides, and manipulated continually along coarse lines of dialogue and thinking.

This process however has very little to do with actual intelligence or merit and even less to do with science. It is like a kind of dogmatic animal behavior in which no one is the winner save stupidity and chaos.

Thus is born the idea of lifestyle communities, or designer communities which are free associations of choice. They offer the benefits of mutual cooperation and mutual consent without the long-term fallout of permanent governments. They offer an alternative to the bloodbath and banality of democracy in its current incarnate form.

The software itself is not the end result; it is merely the arbiter of the process. Even if you were to take away the software, or no matter how many different iterations or themes may come in the future, the underlying principle would remain unchanged. Even without the software, the principle may endure in people's minds. It is the principle of *an alternate way*, and that way is *lifestyle design*.

Lifestyle design fulfills Marx's old saw of "creating the new within the shell of the old."

Capitalism has formed the foundation and the proliferation of both material and knowledge on which the basis of lifestyle design may proceed. The aspirational aspect of *capital*, found in capitalism, in which one has an idea and a dream and hopes to strike it rich, are not wrong. In this, I agree with Ayn Rand: being wealthy is not the problem. It's how to allow the poor and middle class to live happily and peacefully. The rich will take care of themselves, as it were, but not everyone is a striver or a boardroom tiger; not everyone wants to be. Some people just want to live simply and in peace. The binary economy provides an option in which the two sides can be complementary, and, in ways, mutually exclusive. There is no need for struggle. On this point Marx— though he may have aspired to a more egalitarian society, like early physicians with their leeches and mercury — simply got it wrong. As any record of the actual implementation of communist principles will show, they have all failed miserably. There is no need to fight. Let *them do them* and *you do you*. This is the inevitable triumph of pluralism.

Yet again, we hear the refrain, "Democracy is broken, but what can replace it?" This is a question weighing on many people's minds the world over. The evidence is clear and present as to the many cases of influence of money in elections and outright corruption and rigged elections in some countries and places. Yet, democracy, on paper, is the best the modern educated Western mind can conceive to form.

I am not so naive, nor pretentious, to think this book or the ideas contained therein will create a utopian society or cure the myriad ailments now plaguing society. Nonetheless, I still believe it is the duty of every conscious person to advance the state of his fellow beings, and to this end, we have created this endeavor with the hope at least of advancing, by degrees, the human condition—of patching, supplementing, or in some cases even replacing the weak, failing, or outright corrupt elements of existing government or corporate institutions.

Politics, in its current form, cannot build a supercomputer. It could have never built even a simple microprocessor. It has about as much chance as a six-year-old playing in the mud with a stick, because it is really, really, dreadfully inefficient and imprecise and takes as its basis fighting amongst its members to be the most natural form. It is only effective as a kind of limiting mechanism to the accumulation of power, first for the congress and executives themselves, and second for the people. No one actually wins in a standard national scale democracy; they just *don't lose* as much.

Big ships vs. light boats

The big ship of democracy, in many nations, both East and West, is, as we speak, outflanked and outmaneuvered by the light boats of a hundred capitalist corporations.

Before our elected representatives even get around to looking at a bill, there are think tanks and NGOs en masse writing and presenting bills tailor-made by their corporate owners to give advantage to said owners, or at least to not take away their advantage. And their lobbyists, armed with promises of big bucks in campaign contributions and a lucrative position at the company after the politician's term is over, form the so-called *revolving door* of business and politics. Actually, it's more like a cancer, eroding any semblance of actual democracy in our existing "democratic" institutions.

In a lifestyle design community, all members choose for themselves the membership style they want, from a normal democracy type structure, to a meritocracy with predefined rules for governance and advancement, to an open or strict consensus style system. You could even have a kind of monarchy-esque system where the rules are created by a certain person and their descendants. Just be careful who you choose to follow! Since lifestyle design communities are, at their base, just corporations, and since membership in them is *at will,* just like normal employment, you could join one, try it out, and see if its benefits and responsibilities are to your liking. If not, you could sell your shares, exit your membership and move on.

Let's say you have membership in one. You're there with like-minded peers, sharing common beliefs. You've built up your food system, automated what parts can be automated, and recruited teachers, doctors, clothiers, cooks, and people of all kinds and made your community into something thriving. You have shares in the food supply system, the automation system and the community restaurant. Why then would you want to sell?

Of course, like regular corporations, there will be lifestyle design communities that will be managed well, there will be ones managed poorly, and there will be those managed in a mediocre way. This is inevitable, but through the churning, through the turnover of different communities, some winners will emerge, and these will spread, add to their members, form alliances with each other and make the world a more stable place. Because unlike existing legacy capitalist corporations, lifestyle design corporations run in a balanced way. You could say a normal corporation now is like a race car that runs hot. It goes fast, it's exciting to watch, but it burns through resources at an alarming pace, and its engine is tuned so high, to the max it can take, so it destroys itself in the course of running.

This then will create a new breed of lifestyle design entrepreneur, someone who has an idea and a few friends and wants to create something great for humanity, something totally new that does something wonderful and different. What exciting times we are living in! This is the power of Aquarius.

The Inverted Paradigm — a corporation that faces inward, rather than outward

In an ordinary corporation, a CEO assembles a team, and leads them to one goal: creating more and better widgets or widget services and selling them, or investing in widget holdings, generating ever more profit. All the members line up and strive for this pursuit - better, faster, stronger. So, there is pressure put both on quality and productivity—a never-ending rat race of *growth*. This is an *outward* corporation. An *inward* corporation asks: *"How can we all work less?"* How can we all maintain the same or better lifestyle for our members with less and less input? Just as with the development cycles of an outward corporation, products get better and cheaper. In an inward one, lifestyles get better and less expensive to maintain. This is achieved in the same way corporations have achieved it now: through automation and process improvement. In a binary economic sense, this can be called "playing at zero" as opposed to "playing at one."

The goal is perpetual harmony or "near stasis," instead of the current paradigm of endless growth.

The Grand Illusion

To achieve scale in an ordinary capitalist corporation (or what is typically referred to as success), you have to beat all the relevant competition, at least partially or for a limited time within your sphere of influence. You have to beat the competition in your market or define a new one. As one can imagine, the upfront cost of doing this can be high, sometimes enormously high. Yet, that is the first step, to say nothing of long-term survival that faces anyone entering the world of business today.

To achieve success within a lifestyle design community, one only needs to achieve relative harmony among the parts, with even an imperfect harmony being sufficient for sustenance.

In other words, vast swaths of humanity are currently making things harder on themselves than they need to be. But it can be changed. Not only can it be changed, but it can be changed at a lower cost than other available routes.

And not only that, after the process has begun, the advantages compound in favor of the lifestyle designer. Because you are not transporting and marketing goods all over the place, all the cost and waste of that is saved. Since buyers and sellers are both known and in fact the same people, quantities can be made exactly and tailored exactly to demand, and made just in time with almost no waste, spoilage or overage; those costs are all eliminated. Because the cost and details of production are known and transparent, all sorts of improvements and fixes can be made at the will of the community, for ever greater efficiency over time.

Similarly, lifestyle design is inherently much less vulnerable to sudden change than a typical capitalist company. Anyone who has ever been laid-off from a job has experienced this. Everything seems to going well. Your life is humming along, bills are being paid, even your marriage is going well. Then one day, suddenly you get a pink slip. In two weeks, you will be sans employment. The shock of it is usually immediate and drastic and worst of all, unlike being fired, it has nothing to do with your performance. You could have been the finest, most loyal, most productive employee under the sun and still get a slip. Even the company itself feels bad about giving it to you, but there's nothing they can do; they have been hit by sudden economic fluctuation, like an ocean storm, arising out of nowhere. Consumers aren't buying their product, and because other than some "market research," surveys and projected guesswork, they aren't actually in touch with their consumers. Consumers don't tend to like being in that much contact with traditional corporations because for one, they find it bothersome, and two, because they perceive, not unjustifiably in many cases, that corporations will turn around and use that data to screw them or gouge them.

Lifestyle Design may even be *anti-fragile* in the Nassim Nicholas Taleb sense of the word because lifestyle design communities will naturally be popular retreats of refuge when other systems are hit by shock. If the speculative economy is in recession, if there is a war or other civil disorder, if there is a major power outage or food shortage, all these will drive participation in lifestyle design. Even in the absence of these, people may still be driven to lifestyle design because of the nearly limitless possibilities. It is conceivable that lifestyle design will thrive in a variety of climates, giving it strong anti-fragility, especially considering that a UN branch report recently showed the cooperative corporations have a better survival rate in recessions on average than their non-cooperative cousins. In other words, when the economy takes down corporations, cooperative ones (though still very different from lifestyle design) tend to survive better.

Efficient machines vs. inefficient machines vs. very inefficient machines

People can't necessarily always spot efficiency because it sometimes becomes invisible, but inefficiency is easy to spot. Think of the most tiresome, bottlenecked experience in frustration you've ever had, and most will name one institution. You guessed it, *the government*. Some governments are slow and inefficient, especially democracies, which are slow, believe it or not, by design. Let's take the American kind of democracy with its representatives and its balance of power - it's intended to limit and slow people. It intends to slow the ability of people in power to abuse their positions or to become dictators. This is because at the time, the founders grew up in a climate of extreme, particularly religious, persecution. So they wanted to protect people through this mechanism, however inefficient.

Next on the list of *inefficients* is large corporations, things like banks and the like, either encumbered by massive regulation or internal bureaucracy or both; they move like dinosaurs before the comet—big whales that are strong but not necessarily agile.

Corporations, unlike governments, at least have a constant desire to be more efficient but they to are limited by their design. Here an analogy with an automobile may be in order.

Imagine a car that is inherited by a new driver every couple months, and that driver doesn't have to have any real qualifications, beyond popularity, to inherit it. Nor does he have to use his own money for gas or maintenance. He doesn't need to have any knowledge of the car, such as who built it or how it was intended to run. All he needs is the vote, and the key is his. If he wants to modify how it runs, he can, but before he can, sometimes he might know that it needs the oil changed, but a committee will tell him a new type of gas is needed, and that's what his colleagues in the Senate say he must do if he wants their vote. But congress doesn't think so and neither do the voters, so in the end, he compromises, mixes the gas and oil and throws that in the engine. Or maybe he needs to change the wiper blades, but someone thinks adding a banana to the windshield will do the trick, so they compromise with a wiper on one side and a banana on the other! Or maybe he puts whistles on the tires, replaces the drive train with a chain—you name it. Not only did the driver not pay for it, but after his term is over, it will be someone else's problem. You can imagine what shit condition that car will be in. Such a car is the government.

It even gets to the extent that you may have policy writers, or the researchers and admins who work for politicians and sometimes even the politicians themselves, who know what the right answers to a given problem are. They know what will work statistically, or mathematically, or simply what has worked or not worked in the past. They actually objectively know but they cannot put the issue across because of its unpopularity, or the unpopularity of how something sounds when articulated (even the results are sound). So-called "politics" interferes with logic and reason and simple good sense in government. This type of thing gets to the point that bad ideas, ideas that have already failed repeatedly in the past, are put forward again and again. A kind of *recycled bullshit* or you could say like a kind of mental delusion that keeps coming up. It is a kind of *exponential* or *compound* bullshit. Only politicians can achieve this level of idiocy. An engineer working alone could never achieve it.

The Tang Dynasty of China, arguably one of the highest civic achievements in all of human history in terms of governance and systems, to say nothing of art or its many other achievements, actually did have a type of welfare state. They provided for the common welfare of the people, but they did so on the wealth of the state itself, not through redistributionist taxation. The wealth of the state, its gold and other assets, was earning income and they used this income to support the people. The kinds of debtor governments we have now are like a parasite. They are always broke and can't seem to spend money fast enough. When they run out of money, they raise taxes and squeeze people harder. It's plain to see, and it's wicked on the face of it. It takes people's hard-earned money and gives it to others. Actually, that's not what's meant by welfare state, but the modern definition has been twisted by modern politicians and communism. We have accepted such a low standard for ourselves. Just look at these broke robber baron governments! There's an elephant somewhere in this room. Can you find it? A true welfare state is built on the wealth of the state itself, not on robbing its citizens. Heaven forbid modern governments actually make a profit! If they were held to the standard of even a basic corporation, they would be shut down immediately and a new CEO appointed! But alas, democracy is sometimes a lowest common denominator kind of affair.

A true welfare state is people living off the inherent wealth and productivity of the state, not the state redistributing everyone's wealth through taxation. (I.e. the state itself is doing a profitable business in something or has ownership of something - think Saudi Arabia and it's oil - that is profitable in and of itself. This is a true *welfare state.*)

At this point, a person may argue that's just what democracy is, a series of structured compromises. You can't always have what you want. It's just a kind of minimum viable product; it's not *ideal*, but it's *ok*. It's true that it's better than nothing. But I would say the real problem is that the locus of control is too broad. It's too macro. The problem is you can't adjust things specifically enough or precisely enough through the method of politics. Imagine if you were to write a piece of computer software democratically. Anyone could write a piece of code and anyone could vote on what to commit, with some people knowing how to code, and some knowing how to code a little bit, and some not knowing anything about coding. And then, people just vote on what's popular. As you can imagine, the result would be so inferior as to be laughable. But with lifestyle design, you have a very local locus of control. In fact you have as many local controls as you can create. They can be independent, or they can combine through the system of alliances. You have member ownership, so the voting parties, however you want to combine them, whether direct democracy, meritocracy, semi-consensus, totalitarianism, etc., have *skin in the game,* so to speak. At any rate, it's probable through the many possible combinations available that *some group, somewhere* will arrive at an optimal combination of governing factors.

Before we dive further, let's look at some historical examples of what didn't work and why, so we can avoid those same pitfalls as we set about to design our own communities.

8

SOCIALISM IS FAILING

The part Marx missed — the human why and the issue of "who pays for it?"

THE GREAT PLAGUE of communism has ever collapsed, despite some, at first noble-seeming ideals of equality and egalitarianism, under the question of, "Who pays for it?"

Healthcare is a human right, some say, as is education, and there is some merit to these arguments. But remember, these things aren't free. They aren't free like other human rights - free speech for example, really is free, as is freedom of assembly, the right to petition, etc. Medicine, not so much. You need doctors to administer, teachers to teach, staff to organize and planners to plan, architects to build and so on. So, who pays for it? This question has always been divisive. As the famous saying goes, "If you ask the people what they want, they'll inevitably say less tax and more services." With lifestyle design and lifestyle communities, the relationship between voting and taxation, for our example (let's just call it "paying for things," for our purposes), is combined in a smart and elegant way. So, if you're a little more egalitarian, when issues related to healthcare for your community come up for a vote, you can vote to fund those things a little bit more, and as a result of funding those things more, you will own more shares in whatever institution or organization is created by those ballot initiatives, and depending on the rules of your particular community, you may even have more votes in the steering committee of those institutions. There are a lot of ways a community can be run, and the software itself is open-ended.

Let's look at an example of how this might work, using the Aquarius software as an example.

A user would receive a message, as easily as a tweet, saying a vote is coming up, with a link to the text of an idea proposed as well as the cost. After a user votes, that user is given the opportunity to also fund the thing which they have just voted on. Those paying would have their names added to a "steering committee" relative to the thing just voted on and a share proportionate to how much they paid in, very similar to shares of a stock or ownership of a corporation. This elegantly takes care of the democracy/"who pays for it" question. While it allows democratic rule and decision making, it has the ability to grant slightly higher enforcement authority to those willing to "put their money where their mouth is," so to speak. Of course, it could be adjusted within limits, within the founding charter of an organization. Say, for example, "a yes vote requires a least .001 bitcoin, maximum of 6.0 bitcoin investment votes per voter," or something like that. This would in effect limit the power of a given user (member), but it would also allow people who are really passionate about a certain topic to invest more and have more say in that particular topic. It would also eliminate things prone to the phenomenon of "everyone votes for it but no one wants to pay for it." It also combines stakeholders. Owners, workers, and people receiving service (customers) are all combined, so the tendency psychologically is to be more responsible to the thing at hand. You *own* it, after all.

In a typical democracy, let's take the United States as an example, "the people" supposedly control the government, as is written in the U.S. Constitution, for instance, "The powers not delegated to the United States by the Constitution, nor prohibited by it to the States, are reserved to the States respectively, or to the people." And yet, do you really feel it is *your* government? Can you sell your share off? Do you receive a quarterly prospectus telling you how well it's doing financially and soliciting your feedback on its management? Can you even ask the government a question about why they are doing something a certain way and suggest an improvement? Sure, there are town halls and things like comment periods and the like, but one's sense of ownership is vague. Anyways, you get the idea. Unless you're a wealthy lobbyist, your sense of real ownership and control of the government and what it does is diminutive. Save for that masquerade, that grotesquerie of *voting* that happens every two to four years, you have very little control.

For all his ingenuity as a social engineer, Marx fell flat on one major point, and that is *motivation* - the reason people do what they do. He hypothesized that given a certain social structure, if such were put into place by violent revolution, people would inherently fall into a predictable pattern - a stateless and egalitarian pattern, as he so dreamed. Sadly, they did not. Far from disappearing as a functional organ of oppression in the hands of the so-called *bourgeoisie*, the state in actual fact aggregated its power and became even more corrupt and monstrous than before.

Moving beyond Marx, we also see that a lot of socialist philosophies, or various philosophies of human engineering, have fallen flat either on their assumptions about human behavior or on their assumptions about the steps necessary to foment the various social conditions which would allow their particular vision to take place.

What I am forwarding, the theory that I am foisting upon the world to test, is that lifestyle design is a highly powerful, highly cohesive, maximally efficient machine of social organization with high loyalty properties and high ideological resiliency. It is powerful because it takes into account the way people like to organize, the way people naturally do organize and the many differences among how people think and the many different thinking and work styles - in a word, lifestyle - yet it provides a layer, a mechanism, by which they can be interoperable - without violence, without conflict, without revolution, with high stability and with efficiency, sustainability, even pleasure and fulfillment.

So, in today's society, you have banks—local, private, multinational and central banks. You have different central banks in different countries. And people differ in their opinions of how well this system works, and whether they are happy with such a system, and whether such a system is just. But, nevertheless, such a system exists now in the present world. In an Aquarius community, you have the ability to create your own bank, indeed your own *banking system*, accountable to and interoperable to the community itself, and perhaps to the community *alone*. This by itself could change a lot of dynamics of how society is now, of how society exists and is dependent. Because as it exists now, most of the "money" in circulation is in-fact debt. So taken as a whole, the world's "net worth" is a negative number, as absurd as that may sound to people. Of course, logically speaking, the world is inherently worth something, of course. I hope the reader can follow me that there is a logical disconnect here somewhere, right?

In a sense, you could think of this as the ultimate form of protectionism. *The organism has evolved,* so to speak. No longer can they come in with their giant sucking machine, and simply ruin whole communities, indeed people's whole lives. At least, it will not be as easy to do so.

Any system, whether communism, capitalism, religion-based societies like the Amish, and every democracy, functions because of implied (or sometimes explicit) social consent and a currency of perceived fairness. You could say a society's smooth functioning is a mathematical function of its members' perception of fairness. This is also often accompanied by a large middle class. If people don't perceive something to be fair, they resist, they drag their feet, they refuse to participate in either overt or subtle ways. Their little station in the vast mechanism of society grinds to a halt. Taken in aggregate, these conditions are what precipitate a revolution. These conditions are what lead people to dread going into their job on Monday. These conditions lead people to be casual and antagonistic in their studies, and these conditions have become epidemic the world over as we've come to the present time. People feel unimportant, they feel they are being lied to, and they feel they are being screwed. Enter *lifestyle design*.

When a person becomes a truly international citizen, the traditional bonds and authority of state begin to erode and breakdown. No longer bound to a single nation, one experiences the freedom to choose. "To whom should I belong?"

Become a spiritually awakened person and these bonds become even weaker and one's experience ever stranger and more profound.

Carried to their logical conclusions, the ideas in this book may ultimately replace both governments and corporations, or at least lessen their impact. Not through warfare or revolution but through obsolescence.

On the division of the economy into speculative and sustainability layers

On the division of the economy into *speculative* and *sustainability* layers, a person can look at this innovation similarly to the development of insulation. Previously, the only way to heat yourself more was to build a bigger fire, but now you can trap heat, which totally changes the dynamic. In short, a *binary economy*.

On the one hand you have the *speculative layer* (the "1"); this is traditional legacy capitalism, what everyone knows about already, the stock market, trying to make it big as an entrepreneur, sending rockets to the moon, whatever. And everyone sells to everyone and tries to make more profit and be more productive. This is what we already have and it will still exist even after there are lifestyle design communities, but it might be modified a bit, it might be lessened. You could still work in a speculative corporation at the same time as belonging to an Aquarius community, they are interoperable, rather than mutually exclusive. But the problem with it is of course the *"sloshing effect,"* the poor worker running to and fro, now hired, now fired trying to support his family. It can be exhausting, right?

On the other hand you have the *sustainability layer* (the "o"); this is a lifestyle design community, the ultimate *safety net,* a place where you can always have your basic needs met, just by fulfilling your own small yearly quota of labor to the group. A place stable *for life.* A *closed loop system*, that *trades only with itself*. Think about how reassuring that is, you can always come home and there it is. Of course you could be kicked out of a community, but in the author's imagination, this would probably be only for things like major crimes or just refusing to work totally, something like that, not the casual sackings common in corporations. And of course the rules for that event would be defined in the community's founding charter, so you'd know when that was a possibility or not. And you would also potentially still have ownership, so even though you are forced to leave, you would get a little return from selling whatever shares you possessed back to the community. And of course, if you didn't like the community anymore, you could always voluntarily leave as well.

From a sort of quasi-evolutionary perspective, this allows a much greater churn in the development and testing of different ideas of governance and could in fact greatly increase the speed of societal progress as well.

Communism claimed "all power comes from the barrel of a gun," but it was wrong about this. It's power came from people believing in its tenants ideologically. Fascism is much more hated throughout the world than communism, but why? Though communism killed far more through malfeasance than fascism did through force, people still hate fascism more. Why? Because fascism did not have enough of a moral facade of justifiability. Communism on paper sounds justifiable because it argues for egalitarian ends. Though it's means in practice are horrific, people still hold up that "at least we are trying for what is good."

But with lifestyle design, ideas that don't work will quickly be weeded out in the churn of rising and falling communities. They will be discovered and minimized without much harm to the country or overall society. After all, we are not asking you to violently overthrow the government first. Far from it; we are only encouraging voluntary participation of willing participants. Just as anyone is free to start their own business with only a little paperwork, anyone is free to start their own community.

Socialism is failing-ish

What socialism is and what it isn't. Socialism for the purpose of our discussion can be defined as *Marxist creep*. Which is to say, forms of Marxism that have *crept into,* but have not wholly converted, otherwise capitalistic societies. These usually involve some form of *taxation* and *redistribution* of wealth. I define these differently than the so-called *welfare state,* to which I assign the simple definition of a state that uses it's own resources to take care of its people, based on it actually being a wealthy and financially sound state.

Why socialism as a concept exists in the first place

Socialism as a concept exists and is allowed to persist in our minds as a form of social good because of the *perceived unfairness* of capitalism. One of the unfortunate poison pills left to us by communism is this idea, this *meme* of the *rich man as evil tyrant*. The greedy miser of Charles Dickens' *A Christmas Tale*, played and replayed over the generations, that allows us to perceive the redistribution of wealth as somehow fair. Because the perception is that in order to create wealth, in order to become where he is in life, the capitalist must have exploited someone, must have robbed someone, must have driven his workers like slaves (or had actual slaves), must have done something deserving of our mistrust, in order to secure his wealth. So, in an effort at *social justice,* socialism says "Ok, we haven't found you guilty of any crime, we haven't particularly accused you of any wrongdoing, but because you are found in possession of such wealth, we will assume some guilt, somewhere along the line, and we will redistribute, by force, a portion of your wealth to the people, being poorer, from whom, presumably somewhere along the line, you took it. And many people, even as I now write this, perceive that to be fair and just. I'm not going to argue one way or the other on this here, because using the Aquarius app, in a lifestyle design community, this setting is left open. You can decide for yourself the level of redistributionism you want for yourself and for your community. It's a sliding scale, as it were, where you can decide what portion, what percentage you want to give to the *common good*, and how much you wish to let your members keep for themselves. I'm merely pointing out that this is where the psychological justification for these kinds of things, these kinds of graded taxation systems and what-not, come from. Essentially, they come from Marxism, because if you look back at the ancient myth systems of older cultures, you don't see this meme at all. This is a kind of modern myth. The idea of the rich as tyrant and how essentially robbing one person's wealth to give to another is justified. We can call this whole phenomenon the *Robin Hood mentality.*

9

HOW DO WE GET THERE FROM HERE?

"You never change things by fighting the existing reality. To change something, build a new model that makes the existing model obsolete."
- Buckminster Fuller

The Dream Machine

THE POWER of ideology as a memetic organizing principle cannot be underestimated. The most powerful organizing forces of the preceding century have all (pretty much all) been ideological in nature. Capitalism, democracy, communism, and socialism are all at their base, ideologies. There are other ideologies as well, such as religious fundamentalism. These are all things requiring people to believe in them in order to function; it is the *implied social consent* or *social contract* as discussed earlier, with people in their respective societies being punished for their relative deviation from the social norms, whether this takes the form of simple social ostracization, all the way up to actual legal punishment. You could argue that *technology* itself in our modern society is a type of ideology as well, with people believing that technology in some form will solve all of society's problems, and this belief, in some, is open ended, not limited to any specific technology. Thus, technology has transcended being an object and has become an ideology as well, and I would argue, a fairly pervasive one.

People believe, for instance, in *the Internet* as a pervasive social good, and as a centerpiece of education. Recently, people, distrustful of banks, have also come to believe in *cryptocurrency* as an organizing principle and as a monetary philosophy, putting their social trust into the concept of *cryptography* as fairness and neutrality. And these ideologies at their core can become things people believe in as agents of liberation, or as agents of social change unto themselves. Indeed, people already do. There are people who ideologically believe in *open source* programming and so-called *"trustless"* design principles, with some people believing in them as passionately as the religions of old. So, these things have become ideologies. *Belief*, whether viewed in light of modern memetic or historical analysis, is an extremely powerful precursor to action of any kind.

But how do we get from here to there?

Lifestyle design - by being easier than any form of revolution - certainly easier than violent overthrow of the government as proposed by communism - may become a prominent organizing force in the future.

Humans, at their worst, are creatures of *the path of least resistance.* Overcoming laziness is the litmus test of any ideology. Can it motivate a person enough to do *more than nothing*? Through history, all the dominant ideologies *did* accomplish this. They provided a goal and a fruit attractive enough for people to give up their comfort, and even their lives, for it in the hopes of a better world to come, a better world for their children, and so forth.

Modern late-stage capitalism is currently, as has been discussed in the preceding chapters, in the process of eliminating human labor from the *cycle of necessity,* which is to say the minimum provision of goods and services for humans to maintain their existence. To wit, there will soon be a lot of people with not a lot to do, so to speak. Some have proposed *universal basic income (UBI)* as a solution to this problem, essentially providing members of society an automatic paycheck for their very existence, since presumably there might be not enough gainful employment to engage them in productive labor, or not enough productive labor available to perform, to secure for them their basic food and necessities. But UBI, like the *human why* problem that has constantly vexed Marxism in all its forms, may be prone to the same drastic loss of productivity as communism. Essentially, if I'm going to receive a check no matter what, why work at all? Why bother to educate myself? So, you may have vast swaths of society essentially loafing it up on their UBI check. This is the same assertion which, correctly or not, is leveled at existing welfare recipients under the current system. Lifestyle design, as a premise, does not create this *de facto* "everyone is paid automatically" state (though a person could conceivably set a community up this way, using the Aquarius app). It does attempt to eliminate some unnecessary work, and duplication of work, but it also creates, in the models we will examine later, some measures of built-in competition and social accountability, to avoid the Marxist *lowest common denominator* work/effort problem.

Historical Communalism, the Precursor to Lifestyle Design

"There's nothing new under the sun," as the saying goes, so let's review some of the forms of *lifestyle design,* albeit under different names, that were attempted in the past. Most of these efforts fall under the blanket term *communalism,* some operating as entities called *communes.* The most common image that springs to mind when many people hear the word commune is the communal farms that were common in the United States and Europe in the 1960s, recalling images of long-haired hippies living together on farms, raising crops, and wearing tie-dyed shirts.

Of course, indigenous Native American peoples have historically lived, and in some cases still live, on a basis similar to lifestyle design, treating their tribes as single homogenous entities that trade internally amongst their members, being sustainable for many generations without need of outside trade. This model, proven historically sustainable, may indeed be of great interest to the budding lifestyle designer.

The urban homestead movement of New York from the 1960s to the 1990s, in which tenants reclaimed abandoned buildings and took equity in them through a variety of governmental and non-governmental (NGO) initiatives is another example of people, of their own accord organizing themselves and taking action to better their circumstances.

Of course, some nation-state entities do have constitutional or other legal provisions for use of land or even ownership of land through means other than outright sale, such as homesteading laws in the United States or Brazil's unproductive land clause in the constitution, or certain common law provisions in England.

There are also cooperatives that coordinate among themselves to serve a common market, such as the Tuscarora Organic Growers organization out of Baltimore-Washington D.C., thus also achieving one of the goals of lifestyle design: the reduction of duplicated labor.

Lifestyle design is really not something far-fetched. In fact, it is something people are already doing on a certain scale. As of a 2008 statistic, more than 120 million people in the United States are members of some sort of cooperative, whether as simple as a *community sustainable agriculture* (CSA) or a labor union. This number has undoubtably grown by the time of this writing. There are at least over 900 intentional communities worldwide that live according to their own rules and regulations, much like those a person can create with the Aquarius app. These, along with the indigenous peoples of the world, are the pioneers of *lifestyle design.*

Interestingly, what we think of as a normal capitalistic work culture, wherein most workers are employees of a few owners, has not been with us that long. Looking back only about 200 years, the majority of working people were freelancers, farmers, artisans, and merchants. Being an *employee* was seen as a much less favorable position, only a step or two up from indentured servitude or outright slavery—something one would do only if he fell on hard times, and then only temporarily, before going back to being his own boss. Just a short 100 years ago even, 70% of Americans owned their own businesses.

People cooperate for all sorts of reasons in non-corporate ways. There are farmers co-ops, workers unions, consumer unions, and so on, with most featuring some benefit of mutual support, mutual protection, or mutual market—people of their own accord attempting to regulate or control what they see as an unfair or out-of-control system through organic means.

There has also been tried, to moderate success, this concept of a *"free store"* wherein community members contribute or bring in excess items they do not need and anyone can take from the store items they need, for free. But this concept unfortunately does not guarantee or specify a level of reciprocity, so it falls prey to the same attrition as *Small Business Saturday*.

Small Business Saturday is the lesser-known cousin of the two major so-called "shopping holidays," Black Friday and Cyber Monday. The idea behind Small Business Saturday is to patronize those small, local businesses in one's own community for holiday shopping as opposed to large chain retailers. In practice, a person with a limited income goes to shop a small business, finds the prices a little bit higher, as they would be because those small businesses cannot take advantage of the economies of scale. The person hesitates and leaves without making a purchase. The person knows making a purchase will keep more money in the local economy and probably ultimately benefit themselves, but the immediate benefit is not there, and the reciprocity is not guaranteed. What if *that* small business owner doesn't patronize *your* small business in return? It's the same with unions. A person is working in a job with poor conditions, and she knows that joining a union may give her a shot at improved working conditions, so she joins. Then the union goes on strike. As a member of the union, she is urged to participate. She knows that maybe striking can get everyone better working conditions, but Betsy, her co-worker, can't hold out. She's a single mother, and money is tight, so she crosses the line and goes back to work. The strike goes on longer.

Eventually, Sally can't hold either, neither can Rachel. Enough people go back to work that the factory can function, and the union falls apart, or at least loses its bargaining power. This problem is faced again and again by some forms of communalism. Because the members are not mutually reinforcing, or *mutually reinforcing enough*, or because their sphere of influence isn't large enough, they can't hold. But in lifestyle design, the setup of a community can be mutually reinforcing to a large degree, mostly closed, and the members (unlike workers and owners being separate, as the case with unions) do not have an adverse relationship to each other to begin with, because the workers and the owners are the same. Furthermore, they are contractually obligated to each other. She agrees to shop from him, and he in turn agrees to shop from her, so the loop is closed, with less ambiguity and more transparency. Furthermore, it is comprehensive. A lifestyle design community can be sufficient unto itself with little or even no outside input needed.

There have even been historical for-profit and non-profit cooperatives which had variable share systems similar to that available and proposed through lifestyle design and the Aquarius app. Variable being either direct share ownership with one vote per share or share ownership separated from voting with multiple shares allowed but only one vote per member, or something similar to *Class A* and *Class B* shares wherein some types of shares can vote, but some cannot, or where some shares connote *ownership* and others only connote *membership* or *permission*.

But in any case, there have historically been cooperatives of various kinds, communes of various kinds that have attempted to solve the sustainability problem or the unbalancing problem, the *"sloshing effect,"* as it were, of capitalism, whereby labor is flung to and fro by the ever-changing needs of capital, here employed, here again fired, at the whim of market speculation, unable to find root or rest from their toils.

Again, we arrive at this question of how to get there.

The Brilliance of Crowdfunding as an Organizing Principle

One of the most brilliant yet unsung revolutions in economics in modern times is this relatively new paradigm of crowdfunding. *Crowdfunding* is a system wherein people, ordinary members of society, not necessarily professional investors, can come together and contribute money to an idea, concept, location or product (often times a product still in development), with the expectation of some reward, entitlement to, or membership in the product or service soon to be created. It is often a concept that did not exist before, something that, not being a tested idea, could not obtain more conservative institutional backing for its funding, and thus turned to the people, as a kind of preliminary vote and litmus test as to the idea's viability, in advance of time and money being spent on the creation of the actual product.

In actuality, you have achieved two goals: you have tested an idea to see if people are receptive to it, and in the case of there being receptivity, you have at the same time secured funding, and you have secured funding without giving up control of a company to outside investors, or obligating yourself to a bank loan that has to be paid back.

Crowdfunding creates an arrangement that is elegantly simple and direct. I can create a great product or service that you buy from me, but *you pay me for it in advance* (which allows me to create it in the first place), knowing that it is something you want. And then I make it. This solves two crucial problems: it saves the entrepreneur *labor* to create something that ultimately no one wants (no wasted production inefficiency or duplication), and it solves the problem of *funding* via advance purchase. It also gives a sense of the *degree of demand*, so a producer need not make exceedingly more production than she has seen demand for in the initial launch.

I foresee crowdfunding as one of the primary ways new lifestyle design communities are started. Using the Aquarius app, one can create first a personal account for oneself, then create a community, create a *"billboard"* for that community (a kind of conceptual description for that community), choose to set the community as publicly listed or private (invite only), create a *"charter"* for the community, which is like a kind of *constitution;* a legal agreement between the parties involved to abide by certain rules and regulations, and be granted certain rights and permissions, just as any normal contract might do, and ultimately launch and crowdfund, or *crowdsource* (make a pledge of labor), as the case may be, the community.

The *charter* would define things like the rules by which a person can be admitted to, or leave (or be exiled from) the community, how and in what ways shares and ownership are handled, how voting is handled and what voting can change or not change. Can the charter be changed by popular vote or only by the consent of the founders, or can it not be changed at all? What voting structure is in use - direct democracy? Consensus? Weighted meritocracy? How does the share structure work? Are all shares voting? Are some non-voting? Does a person get one vote per share or one vote per member? Under what conditions may a person be asked to leave (forced to sell their shares)?

Using the magic of the *Ethereum blockchain*, the community could create for itself a cryptocurrency or token to use as a medium of exchange to facilitate trade between its members. The community would create a *bank to* issue currency, under certain rules, and assign a banker or bankers *(multi-sig authorities)* or a *smart contract* to run the bank. This could be a few individuals, up to and including the vote of the community as a whole (much like the earlier *DAO* project).

The community could launch with or without pre-created *membership seats (*similar to ordinary corporate job descriptions), which would define, like a job description, what a person's role or responsibility would be within that community.

For instance, the role of *baker* could be filled by Sally. The community would have Sally's resume that tells she knows how to bake pies, and the community could set the price of pies at .004 token each. Flour could be crowd-purchased (group buy) at the beginning of each month, and a kitchen and shopfront provided for her use in the common galley. For her obligation to the community, Sally could agree to bake 10 pies each day, and for this, she would be compensated 1 *token per day* and her obligation to the community would then be fulfilled. The goal within a year might be to have a Baxter robot that would be acquired and trained to bake pies, and Sally could earn 2 tokens a day and check in on the robot once in the morning and once in the evening to make sure he is still baking pies as instructed.

You could do this same thing for a doctor, a teacher, a mechanic, and all other members of the community. Each would have a certain agreed obligation, facilities provided and a price set, etc. In this manner, like a legacy capitalist corporation, the community gains production efficiency over time, thus reducing input labor needed. Compound community improvements over time would result in greater quality of life. Of course, this is only one example; you could manage these variables in a huge variety of ways and the software could store and track all of them.

10

AQUARIUS QUICKSTART GUIDE

"A designer is an emerging synthesis of artist, inventor, mechanic, objective economist and evolutionary strategist." - *Buckminster Fuller*

How to Use the Aquarius App

WHEN YOU FIRST OPEN THE Aquarius app, you will be asked to generate a member token. This will identify you as a member of one or many of the communities you may create or join later.

Then, you will be asked what you want to do:

>> Start my own community

>> Join existing community

>> Advanced crowdfunding community model (still in development)

Let's say you selected "Start my own community."

This community is secret >> shared.

Move the slider to set your community as either secret or shared. This determines whether other users can see your community in the search function of the Aquarius app. You can modify this later.

Next, give your community a name and enter the text of its founding charter. The text of the founding charter could be like a constitution of sorts or it could be a simple shared purpose, forming a temporary community for a given task, for example.

Then, answer the question "Who founds this community?"

Answer by entering the member token public key numbers of the founding members. A ping will be sent to their user accounts asking if they accept their roles as founding members of the community in question. Once a yes response is received from each user, you may proceed to the next step. If a *no* response is received from one or more users, the app will prompt you if you want to proceed without those users before continuing.

Set the rules by which the founding charter and name may be changed, such as:

a. By a unanimous vote of the founders only (strict consensus)

b. By a unanimous vote of the founders plus all members (strict consensus)

c. By a 2/3 majority vote of the founders (super majority)

d. By a 2/3 majority vote of the founder plus the members (super majority)

e. By a simple majority vote of all members

d. By a weighted share ownership vote (at 1 vote per share of ownership of the community's common properties and institutions)

e. and so on...

(These values from the dropdown are pulled from the Aquarius Public Ecosystem Wiki.)

Next, set the rules by which a person may join or leave the community and the circumstances under which a person may be forced out (forced sale of shares).

Note: The word *rules* is used generally here, but there are, in actuality, two kinds of rules in use: *hard rules*, which become part of the code of the community inside the app that governs how it algorithmically functions and how members may interact with it, and *soft rules*, which are verbal or written agreements between humans, subject to community or legal interpretation (non-algorithmic), which are merely recorded for reference within the app.

Next, mint your community's currency by giving it a name and by setting a hard or flexible ceiling on the amount that can ever be created.

a. Hard limit (gold standard)

b. Flexible limit; bank can create more (quantitative easing)

This currency will be created, along with the rules of the community, and the ledger of the community's votes and ownership, etc. on the Ethereum blockchain.

Next, you will set your community's bylaws. Depending on what method you selected in the earlier steps regarding who can change the community's rules, this step either requires a vote of the founders or a vote of the founders plus the community members to invoke it.

This step is large and ongoing and is broken down further in the Aquarius white paper. This can actually be structured in a flexible way by the user, but basically, a user account can attach itself (by mutual permission of both the user and the community) to one or more communities, and a user's status within a given community is called a membership, and it can also store currencies attached to its user number, like any crypto-wallet. Each membership has basic attributes that can be assigned to it, namely rights (which is what you will receive from your membership "responsibilities" (which is what you've agreed to contribute to your community) and voting privileges (which can be tiered and exist in multiple instances).

Communities, in turn, have members, positions (which are similar to *jobs* in legacy corporations), institutions (which are like committees within communities, designed to manage certain functions, education say, or medicine), assets (which are things the community owns), alliances (which temporarily join two or more communities, with members inheriting the respective rights and responsibilities of each), and the bank (a special class of institution overseeing the community's monetary base). Again, these are just basic examples. New classes of attributes can be created and assigned by individual communities as they see fit.

An Example of How Life Works in a Lifestyle Design Community

Jamie woke to the sound of the cock crowing. Groggily, she thought she was back on her parents' farm, but the sight of

Baxter, the lovable coffee-serving robot, roaming the corridor below reminded her she was in Ecotrope, and the sound she heard came from their community farm tucked neatly between their office and residential towers. She rolled out of bed and logged into the Aquarius app.

She was new to Ecotrope, so she was still learning how to use the thing. She saw she had still had 27 coffees remaining to redeem for the month. She also noticed she was scheduled at the educational institute for her weekly 4 hrs of work, in twenty minutes, so she'd better hurry over to the office tower. She grabbed her bag, nudged her floor-cleaning robot, and shut the door to her residential suite.

On her way over to the office, she grabbed a strawberry tart from Samantha, the pastry artist whose shop sat adjacent to Ecotrope's rooftop hydroponics garden, which grew the fresh strawberries she used for her tarts. She scanned the QR code of the shop's display for strawberry tarts, heard a beep and saw a tiny amount deducted from her balance of qmetal, the name of Ecotrope's community cryptocurrency.

She waved to Sam and continued toward the office tower. Her phone plinked and she saw it was a notification from the Aquarius app. A proposal was incoming to create more solar panel arrays on the roof of the residential tower. She saw from the proposal summary that it would cost .000086 qmetal per member (of which Ecotrope currently had 1031 members) to fund the solar array, that a yes vote required immediate payment, and that a yes vote would also grant a member voting privileges in the solar array institution - created in the event of successful funding - and that a yes vote gave a member one share of the array's ownership, should it ever be sold later. The voting would open at 5pm that evening and close at 5pm three days later. She made a mental note of it and continued on.

That weekend, while taking in some Nightflix on her couch, she voted yes on the solar array proposal. Later, she saw the proposal had reached the funding threshold and passed, saw the qmetal deduct from her account and saw the solar committee voting privilege appear in her rights column and the share appear in the shares column of the personal view interface in the Aquarius app. Baxter brought her some espresso. Life was good.

∽

NEXT, you would set the rules by which a person could join the community, the rules by which a person could leave the community and what would happen if a member were essentially kicked out (forced exile, forced sale of shares) and the rules by which this could occur. Aquarius stores such information and displays it to potential joining members in much the same way typical software asks a person to accept terms and conditions upon installation.

Once these basic parts of a community are set up, the Aquarius app can optionally output legal documents that outline in legal terms what the members of the burgeoning community have agreed upon. There is a multi-party contract or a series of contracts between members, depending on the legal framework of the country a given community finds itself in. This helps to "set" the community within the bounds of the law where it physically exists.

For communities whose members cross international boundaries, a kind of "templated" contract can be output on the basis of international commerce law (law of the high seas) or similar, though it will be subject to interpretation depending on which jurisdiction it's in. An example legal document may resemble the following summary, in brief:

∼

WE, the following undersigned, do hereby form this corporation named (community name) for the purpose of (any lawful purpose) in (state or jurisdiction it is in). We, the undersigned, agree to perform the functions of said (member positions in the software smart contract) in good faith to the best of our ability until such a time that our contract is terminated by either us or other parties to the contract (at will). We acknowledge that at such a time, we will be compensated for any shares or assets we had title to under the contract, according to the rules outlined in the contract. In the case of a dispute, we the undersigned agree to abide by the result of binding arbitration under the authority of (community name) as allowed by law.

Example of the Advanced Crowdfunding Model

Jamie was browsing the lifestyle design communities' "now forming" boards and noticed a community called Brightplace. She noticed it had several features she wanted, like 65% override consensus voting with vote delegation, single transferable vote and ranked candidate voting. There were several positions open for teachers, so she decided to apply.

Brightplace was set to launch in 30 days if all the positions were filled. There were positions for a doctor, a mechanic, a chef, a firefighter, a fashion designer, a computer programmer, a librarian, several teachers and security guards, numerous cooks, 3D printer operators, a secretary, a banker, a lawyer, multiple carpenters *and construction professionals and a full-time poet. She saw the English teacher position was open so she applied for that, which also required a $2500 buy-in, payable upon acceptance.*

She saw in the description that once formed, she would be issued 10,000 Brightcoins, the name of the community currency. As an English teacher, she would agree to work at least 16 hours per week for a rate of 40 brightcoins per hour paid directly to her by the bank, plus bonuses for student happiness as expressed in her position's feedback score. She uploaded her resume through the forum's digital portal and crossed her fingers. A few weeks later, she saw Brightplace had commits from 65 members and it had filled all positions, so it would form. They would use the capital they had raised from member buy-ins to purchase an abandoned urban building in which to quarter the community's members and for office space. And *smile,* she had been accepted! It was time for a new beginning...

The initial publicly available builds should be living here: https://github.com/CourtReinland/Aquarius

Updates on the overall Aquarius and other affairs should be able to be found here: https://aquarius.community/

You can support what we are doing here: https://patreon.com/courtreinland

11

SAFE AND STABLE NO MATTER THE WEATHER

The inevitable reaction to globalization

THERE ARE many benefits globalized trade has brought to the world's people. In the way the ancient Egyptian city of Thebes became a cosmopolitan paradise by making itself the center of trade, circulation of goods and the ability to get a rarified gem from Vienna in New York, or art from Italy in Nepal is, of course, not a bad thing. But *so much* trade, especially unadulterated *free trade,* has not been without consequence, not the least of which is the psychological state of overall *uncertainty.* The feeling that the world in some way has become more *fragile,* with some of it certainly being *unsafe,* if not outright *catastrophic.*

Some, though I do not totally agree with them, as their aims are more in league with the communist than I am willing to be, have compared the modern large multinational corporation to a rapist, forcing its way over the boundaries of national law and sovereignty and democratic governance, opening whole countries to its will and pleasure. And there is some evidence to support this. Free trade agreements on their very face subvert national constitutions wholesale, or at least deprecate their status.

Of course the Aquarius software does allow for the making of alliances, even great alliances through its technology. And it allows for departing from those alliances if and when they become top heavy, corrupt, or unsustainable.

Sun Tzu and winning the battle without fighting.

Sun Tzu, in his world landmark treatise, the *Art of War*, stated, "The supreme art of war is to subdue the enemy **without fighting**."

It is clearly seen that this is correct. Obviously, if two people fight for something, to say nothing of two armies, both of them have to expend energy, regardless of who wins. The longer and more prolonged the fight, the less valuable will be the victory and the greater likelihood that the contested thing itself, be it a city or a sweater, will be damaged in the process. Far better if the outcome of the fight, or the process of the fight were limited or set within a certain scope of rules from the outset with both opponents agreeing to abide by them. This, in fact, is what modern political contests have become. When a Democratic candidate bests a Republican at the polls, or Labour gets a few more votes than the Conservatives, they don't charge at each other with swords and lances, determined to hold onto their seat. Although, I may say that might make for far more interesting TV than current politics.

Or when one CEO's earnings report outshines the other on the analyst's chart, he doesn't race across the street to his office, throw down his glove and start loading his musket. He simply takes up the mantle of good capitalist competition and vows to make his company win on the next quarterly report.

The rules by which victory is achieved are agreed upon in advance. Actually, some ancient Native American tribes held to a similar principle, where in combat, if they were able to merely touch, but not kill, an enemy Chief in battle, the other would yield, recognizing his superior skill and realizing a prolonged fight would result in his death.

So, in some ways, the Aquarius software and lifestyle design are just the natural evolution of this concept of agreeing to abide by the rules of arbitration and contract enforcement, by *agreeing to disagree*. From the caveman and his club till now - from spears, to guns, to shouts, to votes, to software. The human consciousness learns to grow and live in greater harmony with its peers.

We as the human race have become more efficient, and we agree to make decisions together that will cost everyone less.

Of course, there will always be some holdouts, some idiots in the mix who just refuse to elevate their consciousness, just as there was probably some dinosaur who tried to strike or bite the approaching comet, even as it was blazing down upon him.

Silicon Valley and the modern tech companies have in many ways already transformed vast swaths of society without a single shot being fired.

So then, as a reaction to the downsides of globalization and modern governmental corruption, lifestyle design is a pretty good one—a good *adaptation* as it were. As a community, lifestyle design communities are fairly self-contained, fulfilling one's necessities 99% within the group and needing only a few baseline commodity inputs from the outside. In the event of catastrophic failure of world food or energy supply distribution, a lifestyle design community could easily have stockpiled vast supplies amongst its members. When it comes to energy, a lifestyle design community could use local solar or wind power and thus be resistant to outages.

Good ideas, under the current system, when forced through the strange machinery of politics and media, are stripped of their nuance and made deformed. Creatures neither fish nor fowl, and lost of their function are trotted out with the most banal elemental dichotomies to PR effect. The oversimplification of concepts beneath even the minds of children (and this isn't giving children enough credit!). Is it any wonder we are in the mess we are in?

The current system is incapable of applied intelligent thought. People know that representative democracy and mass media communication are fundamentally broken, but we are left with a nagging and up until now, unanswered question. What replaces it? If not democracy, what is there? Certainly not communism, totalitarianism, fascism... We have lived through those things and seen their horrors. Certainly, it can't be capitalism alone by itself. Libertarianism? Socialism is what is practiced the world over, but it is the dinosaur body we now inhabit. Democracy sounds great on paper and yet, in its current form, it is broken. It has still failed us, yet we are loathe to admit the elephant in the room because our collective mind has not generated a competent replacement that is not still fundamentally a form of socio-democratic, redistributionist republicanism.

Fundamentally, more people than we would probably like to admit are lazy. We, like the molecules, tend to follow the path of least resistance. Matter, being inert, will remain so until given an irresistible reason to change. People are more motivated by the avoidance of pain than the pursuit of pleasure. It is for this reason that we do not have more billionaires and Olympic athletes than we do. Capitalism wins the victories and achieves the results it does on the back of the pursuit of excellence *by a few*. Work harder, make more money, get more benefits. But what if a system could be found that rewarded increased efficiency with greater ease to the participant, instead of increased benefit for increased output? Wouldn't this create a non-noise pollution and non-junk filled environment? — the zen inverse of capitalism. A corporation that faces inward rather than outward. *A lifestyle design community.* That's the term for what we are doing here. We are collectively creators of designer lifestyle communities.

The three-way struggle of a traditional capitalist company - shareholder vs. employee vs. customer

As we have already enumerated, standard capitalist companies function chiefly for the benefit of their owners, their shareholders. They know in their wisdom that they must serve and create value for the customer or no customer will patronize them. They know that they must pay and fairly treat their employees - at least to a certain extent - or no one will work for them, and they will lack the ability to run their business effectively. Still, the elephant in the room is profit. From a purely efficient engineering or scientific perspective, profit is *waste*, it's leftover capacity or capital that was not needed to turn raw materials into products and services or to pay the people making them. Thus, a three-way struggle is born. If the customer knew how much margin was in the product or service they were buying, they would demand a cheaper price. If the employee knew the profit his labor was achieving, he would demand higher pay or go into business for himself. Of these three tigers against each other, the shareholder eats first and to the employee and customer go the leftovers.

Now, some companies have innovated on this and formed cooperative or employee-owned companies, thereby combining two of the tigers - owner and employee - into one. But the customer is still a fifth wheel of sorts. Lifestyle design does away with this three-way fight by making owner, worker, and customer all the same people.

The advantages don't stop there; instead, they multiply. Major companies spend millions a year doing market research, to learn what people consume before making new products. They have to spend millions because people are leery about interacting with or even taking simple surveys from corporations and brands because of basic, not unreasonable, assumptions that this information will be used to track them, manipulate them, or screw them later. People have developed a love/hate relationship akin to the dependency of an abusive interpersonal relationship with the world's major brands. On the one hand, they don't trust them, but they still crave and use, and sometimes even depend, on the products they create.

In a lifestyle community, the consumers and the creators are the same. You can directly ask people what they would like and directly vote or decide, according to the principles of your community, what will be created. Since people are already connected and at least presumably somewhat on the same page about what type of community they want to create for themselves (or else they wouldn't have joined in the first place), there's no need to advertise either. Since the community members themselves and the communities' means of production (of food, clothing, etc.) are, or at least could be in the same physical location, you don't need to ship items either.

Since they are not residing in multiple locations but instead are made and consumed "on demand," you don't need to store them or preserve them; they can just reside in people's homes or on the community's "work floor." This can be called *compound savings at scale* in the same way that mass production techniques have allowed for products to be made quickly and cheaply and sent all over the world. *Mass interconnectivity* on the local scale is the inverse equivalent for an *inward facing* community corporation to what *economies of scale* was for a legacy capitalist corporation. The reduction in waste, energy use, and environmental pollution are equally dramatic. With things like 3D printers, on-demand textile (clothing) machines, CNC machines for wood cutting, localized organic or hydroponic farming, these advantages are even further compounded. For any raw materials you need from the outside, you can leverage the power of bulk and group buys.

We are essentially doing to the entire manufacturing and distribution process what the desktop PC did to the mainframe and the cell phone did to the desktop PC. We are smaller, faster, lighter, and we do the job better with fewer resources.

12

TOWARDS GREATER HARMONY

∼

THERE IS something very wrong with the world. Communism has failed us. Capitalism, at least in its current incarnation, has failed us. Their bastard offspring socialism is currently limping along into oblivion. The sixth mass extinction is upon us. If we don't do something now, *we will all die*. Modern socialized-democratic-republics are insufficient in both speed and capacity to meet the needs of modern humanity, to stave off environmental calamity, and to allow for universal peace - or at least, not to be overly utopian - the absence of constant war. We are the dinosaurs staring the approaching comet in the face. **We must act.**

To the reader of this book, I would now ask a favor. Think of the universal qualities of truth, compassion and tolerance as you go on. Try to envision them as you read and carry forward with an open mind. If the reader can truly achieve them and embody them in word and deed, I believe there is hope for humanity.

When I watch television, I am stultified. Watching politicians debate things or news anchors analyze them (my pardons to the few good seeds in those professions) is an easy way to become less intelligent.

Advancement can be had by reading books or reading important things on the Internet (by this, I mean not the mindless memes on social media or the distraction of games and entertainment) and by acting. Become first a scholar and then a doer. It is not enough to know; a good person must also act on what they know to be right. If you can, become a creator. But by all means do not list only in the zombified wastes of *consumer*.

Becoming a conscious actor in one's own life and a participating member of the collective world community is one of the joys and gifts of being human. It is my sincere hope that all my readers treasure it and treasure yourself and the chances you have been given. Not all people will act, of course, but it is the actors who can change the world and who will control most of its power.

A Paradigm Shift

The speed of everyday life and the scope and nature of its change has eclipsed the ability of government and therefore law to keep up with it or regulate it meaningfully. It is time for a new paradigm.

I am not a great programmer; I am merely average. I am only a philosopher, but I leave in your hands a blueprint in the hopes that nobler, abler minds after me might fashion a working system by which a community may be built and a lifestyle agreed upon.

I'll say it here but I'm sure people after me will debate it, thus proving my point. You will never get everyone to agree on everything, including this book. Pluralism is the most sensible of the pragmatic philosophical positions and the easiest to implement. All you have to do is let go and not always insist on your own positions. Any one of us may not have the answers, but we may have some. Live and let live.

I would here encourage the reader to look at people's hearts, not labels and names. Liberal, conservative, communist, capitalist, socialist, anarchist, libertarian, religious, agnostic - these are just labels. There are good people with all of these labels who want a peaceful and harmonious world, just as you do.

13

CHARITY IS GOOD, SELF-SUFFICIENCY IS BETTER

THERE IS nothing wrong with helping people. Who would argue with that? But the saying "Give a person a fish, feed them for a day. Teach them to fish, feed them for a lifetime," has never been truer. Some kinds of systematic helping can limit people, make them dependent or even damage them. The best kind of helping resembles raising children. Give them a lot when they are very young, but as they grow, let them come into their own and achieve ever greater levels of independence until they can maintain themselves with no or only occasional help.

This is the main thing, the crux of this book — we have inverted the dominant paradigm. We have created a system that constantly needs less work and less input to sustain itself. It thus frees up human productive capacity for work on greater and ever greater horizons.

14

CLOSING COMMENTS

∽

WHY IS the sense of civic responsibility deteriorating, or in some cases totally gone, across vast swaths of the population? It's because people feel they are being taken advantage of. They feel they are being taken advantage of by their own governments and by large corporate institutions they come into contact with. There's a sense of "Well, they're screwing me, so why should I give them the time of day?"

In some cases, it's real, and people really are being taken advantage of, and in some cases, it's only perceived. But the perception is enough to make people act or *not act* as the case may be. People feel they don't belong to their own communities, they don't particularly care about the place they're from, or necessarily the place they live now. Their circle of interest extends only to their immediate friends and family and in some cases, to their workplace. In the worst cases, it is self-interest alone that drives them.

But there has been in the past, and the hope of this book is that there can be again, a return to what now may seem to be "old world" attitudes. There was a time when craftspeople, regardless of their trade, took their work very much to heart and put their utmost effort in. They felt it a point of pride and were even ashamed when their work was beneath their own high standard of excellence.

Not only are we changing the paradigm of the work/life relationship, but we are changing the paradigm of how change is thought about in the first place. The old paradigm was violent revolution. Don't like the government? Not happy with it? Overthrow it and make your own. Easier said than done, right? It's bloody hard to do and bloody violent as well! But actually, here's the thing, here's the secret - you don't actually need to do that. All you have to do is *not participate*. Don't participate in the things you dislike, and fully participate in the things you do. This is being a conscious person, a conscious *being*. Remove the paradigm of constant warfare, embrace the paradigm of continuous harmonization. Embrace truth, compassion, and tolerance. Isn't that it? Isn't that what the best of the world's great leaders have taught? In fact, it's only waiting for you to put it into action.

∼

IF YOU HAVE an idea and a few friends, you can change your life.

∼

THERE MAY YET COME AGAIN one of those masters of government and organization, like Louis XIV of France or Tang Tai

Zhong of the Great Tang Dynasty of China. We may again see a leader capable of uniting into community a great number. Or we may see small but thriving independent communities as colorful and diverse as the people and personalities that comprise them.

Some people say we are marching toward a singularity, and they talk about the collective consciousness. Well, I am freeing up bandwidth in the collective consciousness. I am throwing the spear at the dragon of Mars and of war and of oppression! We do not need your fake manipulation, your paper tiger and your money and greed for money. Why should all work like slaves for their bare necessities? It's ridiculous! But these are chains of our own making. We've got to outsmart ourselves. I'll tell you there is no oppressor greater than our own minds. If you can think differently, you can change your mind. You can change your life! We do not need these things. Humanity has outgrown these things! And if you can grasp these concepts, you too can step beyond them. Let's all step together to a more glorious future!

∼

ONWARD AND UPWARD! To the Age of Aquarius!

15

FAQS

∽

Q: Do people have to rely this much on technology? Isn't this going in the opposite direction of a simpler life?

A: I'm not favoring a technocratic state. I believe people should spend a large and respectable amount of their time interacting directly with nature and other human beings, not computers. However, computers can play a decent arbitration, neutral record keeping, and accounting role, which is valuable.

Q: Won't such comfortable, sufficient, and indeed almost automatic communities simply make people lazy, perhaps incredibly so?

A: Indeed, there is no absolute guard against this human tendency. Some people are incredibly lazy now in our existing societies. But a study of small group psychology may show, and indeed anyone who has ever lived in a small town can tell you, anecdotally, that this will not be the case, at least no more than in the anonymous tracts of a large nation state or urban city today. The reason? Simple social pressure. No one wants to be perceived as absolutely lacking or lazy. Furthermore, among intentional communities of the willing, people are more inclined to put in even more effort to earn the praise of their colleagues and confederates, their fellow community members. If there are a few rogues, as there is want to be in every group, simple exile from the group, under the defined community terms of such action, may solve the problem.

Unlike certain existing public institutions, with lifestyle design, you don't have to put up with annoying and uncooperative persons indefinitely. You may simply remove them from your group.

Q: What about criminal justice or other legal issues?

A: As corporations and natural citizens under whatever jurisdiction you find yourselves, those laws would still apply to you, and you would still have the relevant protections. On a practical level though, for local dispute resolutions, it would be important for two things to be known:

1. The process by which a person may be added or removed from a community.

1. What constitutes ownership and how a person may buy or sell shares.

In many cases, punitive punishment may not be necessary; simple exile from the group may do. There is an excellent documentary on the Truth and Reconciliation Committee of South Africa. That's one example.

Q: Won't "too many cooks spoil the pot," as the saying goes? And also, "nothing is worse than art by committee." Is it really good to have so many people making decisions?

A: This mostly applies to democracies, other type of republics, meritocracies, and if you want, monarchies wouldn't have this problem. But in the case of a democracy or consensus community, a committee structure may be used. It is impractical to have the whole of the group manage the minutia of certain institutions, so for those cases, even, let us say if a given rule is decided by popular vote, persons at the time of the vote may allocate their own funds to the control of the committee in question. And of course you can elect chairpersons or executives to make decisions on things by proxy, much like a president or prime minister in the current systems.

(The vote decides "should we do the thing?" then the investment on behalf of a group of shareholders decides "to what extent shall we do the thing?" and also "who controls the execution of the doing of the thing?")

Q: What if a community goes broke or just outright fails?

A: There will be communities that fail, that is for sure. There will be mismanagement, politics and simple greed. But the idea itself is a powerful premise, and it is malleable and expandable. Over the reiterations, over time and cycles of improvement, just like normal capitalist corporations, some are bound to get it right.

So, here again, Aquarius is fundamentally pluralistic. It is not and does not claim to be a single right idea. Rather, it is a platform or toolkit, or at its most fundamental, a way of thinking within which all kinds of ideas can be formed. The main paradigm, that of an internal corporation, the inward facing community, is a kind of immutable idea that once released into the wild will breed and evolve until in some form it will inevitably survive. For a community to be a success, it need not be a democracy - it just has to be a sufficiently interoperable efficient structure.

Q: Doesn't this become capitalism all over again?

A: Yes it does, sort of. Of course, lifestyle design never fully abandons capitalism from a philosophical perspective; it just modifies the basis on which it acts. In this case, the *speculative layer* can be seen as an outgrowth or as a flourishing on top of a stable *sustainability layer*, not as a replacement for it, or as a threat to its existence. It is one which, though speculative in nature, is also under the control of the originating community, which can shut off the flow of new tokens or coins at any time.

Q: Is Aquarius a completely trustless algorithm?

A: Trustless, trustless, trustless. You hear a lot of people talking about this concept of trustlessness, putting absolute trust only in cold algorithms. So, people have asked, to what extent is Aquarius trustless? My answer to that is not absolutely trustless, but better than *mean average trust*, and I would argue that better than mean average trust is all you need.

To not trust anyone, when you're talking about human interaction and people living in harmony with each other, is actually a very scary thing. As we saw with the DAO Ethereum hack that happened, we had this supposedly trustless organization, the DAO, floating out in space, floating out in the blockchain, which was supposed to be this grand neutral arbiter of fairness, with the record on the blockchain being law. But of course, there was a hack and about $50-$60 million dollars was stolen, and the Ethereum community decided, over some heated debate, they would hard fork Ethereum, so now you have Ethereum and also Ethereum Classic, which still presumably has the stolen money circulating inside it. Some exchanges still recognize both. Essentially, it was like they split the difference on the trustlessness issue, basically saying we're going to do what's "right," or most people's perception of right anyways, to return the stolen money, but then we're also going to keep the old blockchain and money so as to not let down people who were promised this trustless system. So, Aquarius still has trust and it still has human actors, of course, and it actually has a "manual restore from last known good backup," with light backups of rules and ownership stored locally on people's devices - not the blockchain - but a light local version, which could essentially be restored just by each member manually restoring it and essentially agreeing to rebuild the community from that backup (which would actually create a brand new community and write it into a new record).

Because I don't think you want a world that is so cold you never trust again or so unforgiving you never make a human exception to a mistake.

In the future, especially as AI gets much more advanced, you may NOT be able to entirely trust machines in the way that we do now. Machines may develop self-interest and become untrustworthy or perhaps "partially untrustworthy."

Q: Haven't the Technocrats, the Zeitgeist Movement, and the Venus Project already tried this and not had much success?

A: These are different, and I would like to address them separately.

Some people say *science, science, science,* do it the way that science thinks is best. I, like others, have often been drawn to this way of thinking and having a kind of *idea meritocracy*. But this concept, upon closer inspection, becomes harder to implement in actual practice, because you say science, but then it becomes "science according to whom?" According to which scientists? Which branch of study? What if there is a disagreement or different schools of thought among scientists? So, science itself again becomes political and with some of these other ideas, it's the same situation. I admire the people who built these very much, and I admire the great effort that went into these systems and the care that was put in to truly bringing about a better human state, but I think a skeptic looking at it might still say, "Those ideas look great, but what if it actually doesn't work like you think when you get it up and running?" Right? Looks good on paper, but... by what method can it be changed once it launches? What's the adjustment protocol? Who decides? Right?

One of the enduring merits of capitalism is its admirable "idea playground." You have a new idea, you have something great, try it! Test it! Do it! See if you can make it go, right?

That's exactly what Aquarius is as well; it's an idea-testing playground. Rather than being a single good idea, it's the ecosystem by which many good ideas can be tried.

Q: How are people paid within an Aquarius community?

A: Essentially, this is open ended. You can literally set it any way you like, but I can give you some ideas. One is obviously a fixed salary, like any normal capitalist company. Or, you could just have people keep the money made from the sales of their labor (everyone an entrepreneur), but perhaps an optimal way to set it would be a hybrid of these, which would provide a mix of stability plus performance incentive. This would be a salary plus market rate for a given product, a very similar setup to a standard *base salary plus commission* arrangement at a legacy capitalist corporation. So, a person would have a guaranteed income (stability), plus a portion of sales (incentive). But some would still just need to be on salary because what they do is not a salable commodity that people buy more or less of, but an intangible that benefits the group as a whole;, such people as maintenance engineers and security guards fall into this category.

Q: What about community security?

A: Some members of the community serve as security guards, and these could both keep a watch on theft or things like arguments and fights internally as well as provide protection against outside threats. When it comes to simple things, preventing shoplifting, say, setting up a single video camera in a store may suffice. You could use handheld QR code scanning to transact everything, and you may not even need employees to man the stands. Again, taking advantage of the social balancing pressures of a closed loop community, this becomes "enforcing the rules with no enforcer." Because everyone has ownership, because everyone is there because of a shared purpose or ideology in the first place, and because management is transparent, there can be a greater level of social cohesiveness and trust achieved, to say nothing of the productive gains of such an arrangement. You may see people who are really excited to be there, who are really productive as well.

16

COMMUNITY EXAMPLES

Simple Fixed Basis Model

THE SIMPLE FIXED basis model (SFBM) is perhaps the simplest, "least thought required" model of community because almost everything is fixed from the beginning and all the inputs and outputs are known up front. It may not accommodate growth over time in sophisticated ways, but it is extremely simple to start.

SFBM is a crowdsourced, fixed input/fixed output community whereby the contributions from and benefits to each member are fixed from the beginning. It is perhaps the easiest to understand conceptually as well as one of the easiest to start. It is simply a multiparty contract wherein each member agrees to contribute one set good, at a regular interval, in exchange for receiving (or having access to) all the goods from the other members. Let's say I'm a baker. I love baking; it was my trade before joining an Aquarius community. I agree to make 40 loaves of bread, 30 tarts, 15 apple pies, and 18 pretzels a week. For this, I receive 1300 crystal tokens (my community's currency). Each pie sells for 3 crystal tokens, and each pretzel is one crystal token and a loaf of bread is 2 crystal tokens.

Let's say there's another member and she is a fashion designer. She makes shirts, pants, blouses and dresses in a few styles each, and she agrees to make 5 dresses, 8 shirts, and 2 pairs of socks each week. Each shirt sells for 10 crystal tokens and a blouse for 15, and pants for 7 and she receives 1500 crystal tokens a week for this work.

There's another person who's a doctor, and another a teacher, a shoemaker and so on. The relationship between them looks like one of those diagrams of a crystal with straight lines drawn between all the points in a geometric pattern.

Provided you have all the basic needs of a person covered, such a setup could exist indefinitely, forever with the same output and the same input, in a very stable condition. Such a thing could be very easy on the mind. A person is employed for life and they would also have their basic needs met for life in a perpetual state like this. Furthermore, the hours and outputs are fixed so it doesn't eat all of a person's time. Of course, one may want more out of life, to have more excitement or so on, but that's what the speculative economy is for. That's what *all the rest* of what we have now is for. That's 1; this is the 0.

Think about it. Just with that setup alone, you have sustainability, you have efficiency of resource use, you have a built-in audience. You have community, and you have stability. That's only the start. Even just that would be wonderful for lots and lots of people worldwide. Just that is enough. Now, think of the things you could add to it.

You could store up resources, food, water, and other supplies, like the survivalists do, but at a community scale, a true community of *thrivalists,* not merely surviving but thriving. You could have a couple security guards as members of the group and then you've provided for the common defense. Now think further. You have one person doing one thing, one skill per person. Could robots or machines replace some of those skills? Yes they could, right? You already have things like the Baxter robot which can learn skills from observation. Some Baxter robots have been trained to cook, to sew, and do other things. And there are machines that can produce clothes from start to finish, just load the cloth in. 3D printers, of which most people are familiar, can make many, many kinds of objects out of various materials and some of them now can even make *buildings.* Whole buildings, houses, sheds, etc. can be *printed out.*

So, let's say the community buys a Baxter for the chef and the chef trains the Baxter, so now the Baxter cooks, and now you can get food at any hour of day or night without any additional labour from the chef. In fact, he can even take whole days off and come back sometimes and supervise the robot. But he's still making the same paycheck, because the community controls the bank and the paycheck can be *whatever you want* (or at least whatever was agreed on when the contract was made). The community buys a Sewbo (a type of sewing robot) for the fashion designer and on and on through the various professions. There are even farming and seed planting robots now. It would be impractical for a person to own all these technologies themselves, but what is a $3,000 robot crowdfunded by 100 people, right? Of course some of these technologies are still imperfect and some jobs automate less well than others, but you can think of it like compound interest on labour.

The same technology that enabled the industrial and information age scale of production, now becoming miniaturized will enable *community scale* of worldwide local production. The more you build up in automation over time, the easier everything gets and the less everyone has to work to maintain the same quality. You may even be able to achieve a *free pool* of robotic labour that members are able to draw on with almost zero input. Not absolute zero, but near zero. It may seem like a fantasy but advances in AI and robotics are already making this possible. But the "how much automation?" question is left to each individual community to decide. I'm just giving an example. Not everyone loves so much technology. Some will inevitably opt for an agrarian human and land based approach. A diversity of viewpoints is healthy. It's normal. It would be strange, wouldn't it, if everyone agreed on the same approach? Which is one of the reasons for the whole Lifestyle Design approach in the first place.

17

THE EXCHANGE SYSTEM

The Exchange System

IN THE FUTURE, there may be thousands or even hundreds of thousands of Aquarian communities across the globe (maybe even on other planets). And there will be a need for them to trade with each other, perhaps trading into a common *"crypto-reserve"* currency like Bitcoin or Ethereum. As we've already established, each community would create, at its founding, a common currency, which its members would recognize as common fiat for its transactions. But there would still be the need to go *out* of a common Aquarian currency, at least for the purchase of certain raw materials or specialized equipment. Of course, you could still use the normal national currency of whatever country your community is based in as well. So there would probably need to be one or several Aquarian exchanges, just as there are cryptocurrency exchanges now, wherein a person could convert to common fiat. These would hypothetically list non-voting currency shares wherein a person could purchase the goods or services available from a certain community without being a member or having voting privileges. Of course, other types of exchanges could list whole memberships for sale, whereby upon sale and approval by the community, a person would inherit all the rights, privileges and shares owned by the person selling.

But now the reader might be raising a question, *"But wait, how is that any different than capitalism and stock exchanges now? Won't that open it up to speculation, and defeat the whole purpose?"* The answer is *yes, it could,* but the community is still in control. They could release very little currency to the exchanges or none at all, instead relying on periodic fiat investment by members to sustain themselves. They could also open and close the supply and availability selectively to achieve the desired result. Of course, the value of a given communities currency is only based on the inherent stability and desirability of that community — how the goods and services are, how the lifestyle is, how well the bank manages its distribution and so on. There would be no point to speculate in it without putting energy into the community itself, because the currency does not have inherent value. Lifestyle design is like capitalism on a different basis, not the elimination of capitalism entirely. It has certain stability, sustainability, efficiency, flexibility, and creativity advantages. You can think of it like the difference between raw iron and steel or other refined alloys. You still have iron inside, but you've limited, mitigated or changed some of the original disadvantages.

I envision a cosmopolitan world of travel and discovery wherein people may hop a plane or hyperloop not knowing what new sorts of hidden communities and treasures their destination will contain. Going somewhere, converting down to the local currency, sleeping in a community member's bed, Airbnb style (for she is also traveling to far-flung communities), eating the local food and enjoying oneself. All the while knowing that one's home, family and community are safe where you left them. We have been sold for ages the "lifestyle" by magazines and television. But it has been a lifestyle based only on consumption, on *one-way* participation: *buy this, wear this, go here, live the lifestyle.* But it was all *faux*, the trappings only, not the actual lifestyle. Now we have within our grasp the ability of *actual lifestyle,* of lifestyle design. I have given you a kind of construction kit. Build on it your dreams.

∽

18

POST SCRIPT

∽

THE READER MAY at different times in the future be unable to find the software to which this book refers. Do not be afraid, many are the forces allied in this world who do not wish to see this book, indeed who may intend on it's destruction and may have used all manner of tricks to obscure or bury the code. Do not fret, it is not so complicated. It is written in Vyper Ethereum which is to say, similar to Python and can easily be re-written in that language. Anyone can recreate it, the ideas are all spelled out in the book. You can even use pen and paper to recreate the ideas, they are after-all only ideas. So long is the method is stable, and open source, and the participants hearts are honest or at least aiming to be so, all should be well. You may not be able to find me in the future, or I may have been de-famed, discredited by this or that accusation or the other. Such are the methods of those who would oppose this. None-the-less, do not let it deter you, would-be builder! People, of course, can be stopped, but trying to stop an idea is like trying to un-ring a bell. You may smash the bell, but people still heard it ring.

CPSIA information can be obtained
at www.ICGtesting.com
Printed in the USA
FSHW020641220219
55835FS